A WRINKLE
IN THE
LONG GRAY LINE

WHEN CONSCIENCE AND CONVENTION COLLIDED

A MEMOIR

BY CARY DONHAM

Cover Art By Susan Cornelison
Cover Design By Marissa Kephart

Isbn: 978-1-66787-432-6 (Soft Cover)
Isbn: 978-1-66787-433-3 (Ebook)

Rogers/Tyner Publishing Co. Llc

Poorly shod and poorly clad, they march away [to war] beneath his

banners, ofttimes with no better arms than a sickle or a sharpened hoe,

or a maul they made themselves by lashing a stone to a stick with strips

of hide. Brothers march with brothers, sons with fathers, friends with

friends. They've heard the songs and stories, so they go off with eager hearts,

dreaming of the wonders they will see, of the wealth and glory they will win.

War seems a fine adventure,

the greatest most of them will ever know.

Septon Meribald in "A Feast for Crows," Book 4, Game of Thrones, p. 533.

CONTENTS

PROLOGUE ix

INTRODUCTION xiii

PREFACE xvii

Chapter 1

Why Did I Go to West Point in the First Place? 1

Chapter 2

Navigating the Draft 17

Chapter 3:

Where Was Vietnam and Why Were We in a War There? 21

Chapter 4:

Beast Barracks 31

Chapter 5:

Getting Down to Business 47

Chapter 6:

Football Season Ends with No Sugar Bowl 59

Chapter 7

One Semester Down, One to Go 67

Chapter 8:

Camp Buckner: The Best Summer of a Cadet's Career? 73

Chapter 9:

Yearling Year 81

Chapter 10:

Diving into the River—The Spirit of the Bayonet Returns 89

Chapter 11:

A New President, a New Strategy, the Same War 95

Chapter 12:

What Next? 101

Chapter 13:

The Army's Hearing Officer Denies My Application for Discharge 121

Chapter 14

The Aptitude Board Hearing 135

Chapter 15:

We Go to Court 147

Chapter 16:

Things Go from Bad to Worse 159

Chapter 17:

My Appeal Is Successful 169

Chapter 18

Life Gets in the Way 181

CONCLUSION 193

ACKNOWLEDGEMENTS 196

ABOUT THE AUTHOR 198

APPENDIX 1 199

Application For Discharge 199

APPENDIX 2. 211

District Court Decision.. 211

APPENDIX 3. 228

Appellate Court Decision 228

PROLOGUE

When Russia launched a full-scale attack on Ukraine on February 24, 2022, many, including, I believe, Vladimir Putin, thought this would be a short battle that Russia would wrap up in a week. However, I thought to myself that this was a fantasy, and I was right. More than five months later, there is no end in sight to the war. From news reports, the war is a daily slog with Russia claiming it controls the far eastern part of Ukraine, and Ukraine claiming it is closing in on retaking Kherson, a city in the south of Ukraine that was the first city Russia captured.

Meanwhile, Russia has implemented a brutal terror campaign against Ukraine civilians, including children, reminiscent of similar "ethnic cleansing" type operations in Kosovo, Rwanda and Somalia, not to mention Germany's holocaust in World War II. And Russia has raised the specter of using nuclear weapons.

Worldwide, the war has increased food shortages because both Ukraine and Russia are major producers and exporters of grain. Russia has effectively blockaded Ukraine ports while sanctions on Russia's economy make shippers and even insurers reluctant to ship Russian grain. Even a spark of hope that was raised earlier this week of a deal arranged by Turkey and the UN with Russia and Ukraine designed to allow both countries to export grain may have been shortlived after Russia immediately hit the Ukraine port of Odessa with missiles aimed at civilian targets the day after the grain export deal was announced.

While the US is not directly involved in the Ukraine war, that war has taken a toll here as sanctions on Russia have raised the price of oil (until recently) causing fuel inflation here and around the world. The US is spending heavily on the war, arming Ukraine with more sophisticated and lethal long-range weapons. Perhaps the only people benefitting from the war are the defense contractors who are producing the artillery and rockets we are shipping to Ukraine.

And recently, Nancy Pelosi's visit to Taiwan led China to protest the visit by carrying out military exercises close to Taiwan. This sequence of events has raised tensions between the U.S. and China, the two most powerful countries in the world. If China decides to annex Taiwan by military force, will that lead to another war, and will the U.S. feel compelled to directly assist Taiwan?

Countries never seem to learn. The USSR invaded Afghanistan and ended up bogged down for years in an unsuccessful struggle that raised Osama bin Laden's influence (with the help of the US). The sad tales of the French and the US in Vietnam should have been a warning to Russia, not to mention the disastrous US invasions of Iraq and Afghanistan. All these military operations beg the question, now that we started this mess: How do we end it?

It brings to mind the Uncle Remus story about Br'er Rabbit and the tar baby, sometimes wrongly described as racist. It isn't. It is a story of resistance, derived from African–American folk tales, with Br'er Rabbit being the alter ego of enslaved African–Americans. As usual, Br'er Rabbit was running circles around the physically dominant Brer Fox, and Br'er Fox came up with a plan to end Br'er Rabbit's mischief. Brer Fox found some tar and turpentine, and created a doll shaped from the tar, put clothes on it and placed it in the middle of the road. Br'er Rabbit bopped along the road while Br'er Fox "lay low" in a nearby ditch. When the tar baby ignored

Br'er Rabbit's greeting, Brer Rabbit decided to teach the tar baby a lesson. He started punching and kicking the tar baby and soon was stuck tight as Br'er Fox rose gleefully from the ditch, finally in control of Br'er Rabbit. Ultimately, Brer Rabbit escaped, convincing Br'er Fox that the worst he could do to Br'er Rabbit was to throw him in the briar patch, where Br'er Rabbit, at the end of story, gleefully shouts he was "born and bred."

Wars are like the tar baby. Once they start, countries start kicking and punching, increasing military aid, sending more troops, building more weapons and suddenly realize they are stuck. But so far, no one has found a briar patch to escape to. Pride, nationalist fervor, public opinion, fear of looking weak, and similar factors become overriding concerns even as the original rationale for the war fades away. Witness Russia in Ukraine, which originally made clear its desire to make Ukraine part of Russia, and now seems to focus only on two eastern provinces it has been fighting in for nearly a decade; or the US in Afghanistan, which after twenty years accomplished little, yet its exit proved harrowing and deadly.

INTRODUCTION

The August 6, 1970, front page of *The New York Times* contained a startling headline: "West Pointer Seeks Discharge as Conscientious Objector."[1] It was startling because a conscientious objector, by law, had to be opposed to all wars. On the other hand, a West Point cadet was training to be an officer in the United States Army, which has a mission to engage in war on behalf of the United States. So how could that West Point cadet—me—be opposed to participating in war?

In 1970, I had just finished junior, or "cow," year, class of '71, in the top 10% of the class academically and viewed as average militarily. I was in the "boarder's ward," where cadets who were leaving due to either choice or academic failure stayed for a few days while being processed out, and ate their last meals at the hospital. I was not being discharged for violating the Cadet Honor Code—a cadet shall not lie, cheat or steal, or tolerate those who do. I was not being discharged for disciplinary reasons. But I was quarantined from other cadets because I had arrived, over my three years at West Point, at deeply held religious beliefs that war is wrong. These beliefs led me to be the first West Point cadet, and to date the only West Point cadet, to seek conscientious objector status.

My soon-to-be first-class (senior) classmates were either touring Army bases or running Beast Barracks, the training program for "plebes,"

---

1 https://www.nytimes.com/1970/08/06/archives/west-pointer-seeks-discharge-as-a-con-scientiousobjector-west-point.html

or incoming freshmen. Plebe is derived from the Latin "plebeian," for the lowest class of humans, only slightly below dogs. I alone among the nearly 4,000 cadets was sorting mail, by order of the Commandant of Cadets, fraternizing for eight hours a day with enlisted men and living by myself in a barracks that during the previous school year had housed about 400 to 500 cadets. Because I publicly opposed war—the version at that time being the Vietnam War—the West Point administration treated me as a military pariah, possibly contagious, who needed to be isolated from the other cadets and incoming plebes. I could not eat in the cadet mess hall and was consigned to eating at the hospital with cadets who were quitting or had flunked out. West Point officers apparently were concerned that I could transmit my anti-war views by osmosis to new cadets or my class-mates who were training them. An internal West Point memo in June 1970 discussed how to make sure I had "minimal contact" with Beast Barracks and new cadets. In fact, they made sure I had no contact.

On the one hand, West Point and the Army claimed my beliefs were not sincere, and therefore, I did not meet rigorous standards for being a conscientious objector. On the other hand, although my beliefs allegedly were not sincere and there was no dispute that I ranked in the middle of my class in military aptitude, I had no aptitude for military service merely because I, apparently insincerely, claimed conscientious objector status. And, as West Point graduate Lucien Truscott IV pointed out in a *Village Voice* article, although West Point said my beliefs were insincere, there was no effort to claim I had violated the Cadet Honor Code by lying.[2]

---

2 Interestingly enough, West Point and its honor code were again in the news in 2020. Re-tired Major General Paul Eaton graduated from West Point in 1972, commanded the army infantry center, and trained Iraqi troops. He criticized Secretary of State Mike Pompeo and acting Secretary of Defense Mark Esper, both of whom graduated from West Point in 1986: "What is wrong with West Point class of '86? Who mentored you? What happened to the West Point honor code in your class? America is very badly served by these men."

So, as artist and musician David Byrne has said, "How did I get here?" This question is still relevant today. Just think about the controversy over whether the recent withdrawal from Afghanistan after 20 years of war there has been a success or a failure, or whether the outcome of that war justified the $2.3 *trillion* cost and the loss of more than 6,000 lives of United States' service members and contractors. So let me try to explain how a seventeen-year-old who grew up in a military town came face to face over three intense years with his religious upbringing when confronted with teaching other young men that the spirit of the bayonet was "to kill."

This is my story of how fifty years ago, as a West Point cadet, I took a stand against war.

I had hoped that my stand, which made headlines, might influence how our country views war. Given the uncertainty in which we live, I firmly believe this story is still relevant. I hope this story opens some hearts and minds to the moral and ethical irrationality of war.

PREFACE

"War is young men dying and old men talking."
—Franklin D. Roosevelt

CHAPTER 1

WHY DID I GO TO WEST POINT IN THE FIRST PLACE?

West Point has had some notable failures. Edgar Allan Poe suffered there for a short time in 1830–1831, before he stopped going to class, parades and mandatory chapel. Not surprisingly, Mr. Poe was dismissed, probably for the good of all of us.

George Custer, who at least one writer[3] has described as the worst West Point cadet ever, graduated last in his class of 1861 and was court-martialed shortly after graduating for neglect of duty. Of course, he went on to notoriety at Little Big Horn.

The painter James Whistler, son of a West Point graduate, also comes to mind. Apparently, Mr. Whistler was smart enough to pass most subjects without much work, and his roommate said that he was "one of the most indolent of mortals. But his was a most charming laziness, always doing that which was most agreeable to others and himself."[4] As you might guess, indolence is not highly regarded at West Point, and after Whistler referred in a chemistry class to silicon, a primary component of sand,

---

3 https://www.historynet.com/west-points-worst-cadet-george-armstrong-custer.htm
4 http://thehistoryinsider.blogspot.com/2012/04/painter-james-whistler-west-point.html

as a gas, his military career was doomed. He eventually was expelled by Superintendent General Robert E. Lee (yes, that Robert E. Lee, the future Confederate general).

I mention these notable failures not because I have been as successful as Poe as an author or Whistler as a painter, or as big a disaster as Custer as a General. However, I managed to generate a good deal of notoriety when I left West Point due to my request for conscientious objector status.

You wouldn't be the first person to ask me, "If you were a conscientious objector, why did you go to West Point?" In fact, my wife read about me in a newspaper article when she was in high school, before ever meeting me, and later told me she'd asked herself, "What kind of idiot would go to West Point if he is a conscientious objector?" It is a reasonable question. It is well known that West Point has always been intended to create elite military leaders from raw, cocky high school boys (and now girls). It has produced some of our country's most prominent military leaders: Generals Ulysses S. Grant, Robert E. Lee, William T. Sherman, "Stonewall" Jackson, John J. Pershing, Douglas McArthur, George Patton and President Dwight D. Eisenhower (not to mention Duke basketball coach Mike Kzyzewski, who I saw play under then-West Point basketball coach Bobby Knight). At the same time, our country had been sending "military advisors" to Vietnam since at least 1960 and increased its troop level there from 1966 to 1967 by over 100,000 to 485,600 military personnel.[5] The war was on TV news every night in 1967. So, if I was a conscientious objector, what was I thinking?

The answer is long and complicated, but it is directly related to the fact that we and every country send our young and often naïve men and women to the battlefront, not the decision makers who decide to go to

---

5 https://www.americanwarlibrary.com/vietnam/vwatl.htm

war. In addition, the sad fact remains that our country and most countries spend far more research, analysis, and money on how to make war rather than on how to resolve differences in more constructive ways. Sadly, the fifty-plus years since 1970 have not changed this.

A MILITARY FAMILY

The oldest of four, I was born toward the beginning of the baby boom, on November 11, 1949—Armistice Day. My father grew up in East St. Louis, Illinois. His father had died when he was seventeen, and his mother, Myrtle Pearl Donham, got a government loan to buy a small confectionary, leading her to becoming a lifelong Democrat. She was a founding member of the East St. Louis Women's Democrats and once rode in a car with Eleanor Roosevelt. She also was a dedicated churchgoer, usually Methodist, which at the time was fervently anti-Catholic. Her political views won out and held true when John F. Kennedy, a Catholic, ran for president. I guess she ultimately decided that a Catholic Democrat was better than the Republican, Nixon.

My father joined the Army Air Corps in World War II, even though he could have received a deferment since his father had died and his older brother had suffered a serious chemical burn injury working at a Monsanto plant and was incapacitated at the time. After training in Texas, he became a pilot in the Pacific theater, in places like New Guinea, the Philippines and Australia. He flew a C-47, known as the "biscuit bomber" because it transported supplies to troops stationed on the front lines. He had 200 hours of combat flying, was a squadron commander and was awarded the Air Medal, given for "heroic or meritorious achievement while participating in aerial flight." He never talked much about the war.

Postwar, my father finished college, earning two bachelor's degrees— one from Indiana State and the other from Washington University in St.

Louis—as well as a master's from Auburn, all on the GI Bill. My father loved all sports, but baseball was his first love. He was a southpaw who played first base for semi-pro teams in East St. Louis when he worked for the Swift packing plant, and in college at Indiana State and McKendree College, a small Methodist college in Lebanon, Illinois. He suffered a severe knee injury, torn ligaments, I believe, playing baseball at Indiana State. Today, these are repaired with minimally invasive arthroscopic surgery, but his procedure gave him a long, ugly scar on his knee, limited his ability to run and ended his career as an athlete.

My mother grew up in a poor family with nine kids in rural southern Indiana close to the Wabash River. I didn't realize just how poor her family was until my wife, Becky, and I visited the graves of my mother's parents, my grandparents, Emmett and Florence Clough. They are buried in the cemetery at Darwin, Illinois, which is barely big enough to be called a hamlet along the Wabash River south of Terre Haute, Indiana. We found the graveyard but didn't know where the graves were. Someone pointed us to a tiny, weather-beaten house down the road. We knocked on the door and a young man, maybe twenty years old, came to the door in a woman's slip. He may have had Down syndrome. He invited us into a living room with a threadbare carpet that reeked of urine. As the wait for his mother approached several minutes, Becky and I started to get nervous, with the "Deliverance" banjos ringing in our heads. Finally, an elderly woman appeared and we explained we were looking for the Clough graves. She said, "The Cloughs? They were dirt poor!" Becky and I looked at each other—if this woman described my mother's family as dirt poor, what would that have been like?

After high school, my mother moved to Terre Haute to attend a "business school" to learn to be a secretary. She enlisted in the WAVES (Women Accepted for Volunteer Emergency Service—the women's branch of the US Naval Reserve) during World War II, and perhaps her greatest disappointment was when she was disqualified from serving due to a "heart murmur."

However, the heart murmur did not keep her from reaching ninety-four before she passed away. My mother was brought up as a strict Baptist. She believed in God—that Jesus died for our sins, that hell was waiting for those who didn't believe and that the Bible was a rule book. She also believed in "spare the rod, spoil the child." Believe me, I was not spoiled. She felt it was her duty to teach her children the gospel and did her best to impart her beliefs to her family, with varying success.

My parents met after World War II in Terre Haute, at a USO where my mother was volunteering, while my father was attending Indiana State. My parents did not talk about their courtship with me, except that my mother would occasionally mention my father's green eyes with a rare smile. They were married in 1948. My dad became a teacher and turned his love of sports into a coaching career. When I was born a little more than a year later, he was teaching and coaching in Bunker, a little town in the Ozarks in southwestern Missouri. From there, my father moved to a teaching and coaching position in Chambersburg, in the "belly" part of Illinois, west of the Illinois River. Then we moved again, when I was about three or four, to a slightly bigger town, Meredosia, right on the Illinois River. Our house was close to a railroad track. Across the track was a vacant field that bordered the river. I played with wooden blocks and pretended they were the barges passing by. At Meredosia, my father received press attention in the small-town newspapers after he punched out a referee who made a bad call that cost his high school team a win. While we lived there, when I was three, my brother Mark was born in Jacksonville, the nearest town with a hospital. We have been close our entire lives. When I was four, we moved again to a slightly bigger town, Glasford, about twenty miles from

Peoria. In Glasford, we lived in two different houses and my cocker spaniel puppy Susie got run over by a motorcycle. I started first grade in Glasford in September 1955 when I was five, although I missed at least two weeks of school when I got the measles. Then, right after school ended, I had my tonsils removed.

Peoria was a big city to those of us who lived in nearby small towns. Among other things, it had an airport. Once or twice, we drove there to watch the planes. One time, while we were looking at planes taking off and landing, there was a young boy with his parents nearby who happened to be African–American. I asked my parents, "Is he black or brown?" My mom quickly shushed me. It was my first experience with race. To drive twenty miles from Glasford to Peoria just to watch planes take off and land, my father must have had a restless memory of giving up being a pilot. I wondered why he chose to leave flying behind since to me it seemed more interesting than being a teacher in a small town.

In the summer of 1956, my youngest brother, Samuel Dean, was born in St. Francis Hospital in Peoria. At the same time, I was in the same hospital having my tonsils removed. The nuns who ran the hospital would not let my mom visit me while we were both there. That same summer, we moved to New Baden, Illinois, a small town about thirty-five miles east of St. Louis on the Clinton County side of County Line Road that separated Clinton and St. Clair Counties. It was a slow three-hour drive with a six-week-old baby, six-year-old and three-year-old boys and no air conditioning in an old Studebaker. I am sure my grandmother Myrtle helped engineer this move, since New Baden was near East St. Louis where she lived, and my mother did not like it. Clinton is a rural county, strongly Republican, of mostly German ancestry. As far as I know, its most famous resident was Red Schoendienst, the former Cardinals second baseman and manager, whose sister worked at the Western Auto store in New Baden. There were no interstate highways at the time, and it took about an hour to drive to St. Louis. South on Route 160, about four miles, was New Memphis, which to my eyes was barely a town. North five miles was Trenton, a slightly bigger and more affluent town than New Baden, it seemed to me, since it had a restaurant and a movie theater.

When we moved to New Baden, my father was to teach and coach at New Baden High School, whose mascot was the Zebras. I thought the mascot was cool, but it was short-lived. Shortly after we moved there, in 1957, either the taxpayers or some bureaucrat created a consolidated school district made up of Trenton, New Baden, New Memphis, and the rural area in between in west Clinton County (hence, the clever name Wesclin). None of the three towns had as many as 2,000 residents then. The mascot became the Warriors, presumably for alliterative purposes.

At six years old, having left behind friends a couple times already, I thought New Baden would be another temporary stop until my father moved on to a bigger town and a bigger school.

I expected to keep moving as I had done the first six years of my life. It turned out I was wrong.

A MILITARY TOWN

In New Baden, I felt like an outsider. In Chicago, where I lived for forty-one years, we have a saying: "Don't send me nobody nobody sent." In New Baden, it was "Don't send me nobody who isn't related to someone who has lived down the block for generations."

New Baden had no stoplights or restaurants, but it did have at least half a dozen taverns and three churches. More importantly, it had a distinct military culture. It was nine miles from Scott Air Force base, at the time a major facility under the protection and encouragement of Representative Melvin Price. Our next-door neighbors were military. Major "Pappy"

Weaver and his family lived across the alley. A Lt. Colonel lived down the street. Two of my best friends' parents were civilian employees at Scott. The military was a normal and accepted part of my life.

Since military personnel tended to be transferred every few years, this meant that some of my school classmates were somewhat transient. On the other hand, most of the rest of the students were lifelong New Baden residents. I rested uncomfortably in between both groups.

I was an outsider to begin with since I had no relatives in New Baden. But as the son of a teacher, I was doubly an outsider, and that was only the beginning, because my dad was a coach. Sports were one of my dad's organizing factors, and all of his children followed in his steps, except maybe for Dean. He was one of the coaches of one of the first four Little League baseball teams in New Baden, and I was assigned to his team. I was a decent athlete, but I always felt other kids suspected favoritism. Even when I was not on a team my dad coached, there was that spillover that put me on the outside.

Another way I was different was that I was an avid reader. I persuaded my parents to buy me what now would be called young adult books about fictional high school and college sports figures, and I read all the books in these series. There was Bronc Burnett, a high school football and baseball player from Sonora, New Mexico. I spent some time trying to locate Sonora on a map of New Mexico—after all, Sonora's rivals, such as Deming and Las Cruces, were on the map, so why not Sonora? I finally figured out that it was a fictional town. There also was Chip Hilton, a three-sport college athlete, and Herb Kent, West Point fullback. This last book, written in 1936, made no effort to portray West Point life. Reading it, West Point seemed like any other college, except it had a really good football team.

As I grew older, my reading expanded. I started taking out Perry Mason mysteries from a library in Mascoutah, a slightly bigger town about ten miles from New Baden. Those novels likely influenced my choice of career many years down the road. My dad introduced me to James Bond novels by telling me that President Kennedy liked Ian Fleming's character, so I had to read them too. I also read books from the *Time* bestseller list, one being *Hawaii* by James Michener, which was an early introduction to sex as well as a long and fascinating story. When New Baden got a library of its own, I took out *Catcher in the Rye*. My mom was furious. According to her, it was a dirty book—but since she had never read it, I don't know how she reached that conclusion. My dad intervened, and I read it anyway. My unspoken thought was that if *Catcher in the Rye* was dirty, what would she think about James Bond or James Michener?

You can look at it as an opportunity or a burden, being smart in a small school. I played cornet in junior high and high school band and at one point was pretty good. I played all four sports Wesclin Senior High participated in—baseball, basketball, tennis, and golf—and lettered in all four junior and senior year. In the ninth grade, I was dragged into being the debate partner of a high school senior and ended up in the middle of a tug of war between the speech teacher and the band director about whether I would go to a debate tournament at University of Illinois or play in the band concert. I ended up doing both, but neither as well as I could have without the drama.

I also became involved in the Civil Air Patrol (CAP), the co-ed official auxiliary of the United States Air Force, which had a chapter at nearby Scott Air Force Base. My neighbor, a major, was one of its local sponsors. It had a military organization, with ranks that were earned like Boy Scout's badges. CAP meetings became part of my routine. The program involved learning military close order and marching drill as well as historical education about the Air Force and the opportunity to win engineering scholarships to college. By the time I left New Baden, I had advanced to a cadet

Lieutenant Colonel. During the summer before my high school senior year, the Civil Air Patrol selected me to attend an Air Force sponsored spiritual life conference near Asheville, North Carolina, where I learned of the intersection of the military and religion—at least Christian religion—Asheville being near Billy Graham's home. At the time, I felt no conflict between the two.

The military culture of New Baden included the Memorial Day parade with the junior high and high school bands marching down the main street past the Hempen Funeral Home, the Post Office, Hempen Hardware, the Frosty Whip and the IGA grocery store. A wizened veteran, marching in full uniform and wearing a garrison cap, was known for his cry each year: "Anybody got a Kodak?" After the parade, my friend Terry Brinkman and I, who also played cornet in the band, were whisked off to the cemetery to play taps after a color guard of veterans fired their salute to New Baden's fallen soldiers. One of us would be near the color guard and would start the call; the other would be stationed a couple hundred yards away behind a tree and would play an echo.

A CHURCH-GOING TOWN

During my preteen years, my mother was the parent who emphasized religion. Despite her Baptist upbringing, we attended the New Baden Methodist Church, a modest wood-frame building with a sanctuary and a basement with a kitchen. Later, my father joined the church and became its lay leader; my mother was the church treasurer.

Every Sunday we walked a block and a half to the church to attend service and Sunday school. It was a small church, leaning toward fundamentalist, and I have always thought that the primary reason we attended it was because there was no Baptist Churches in New Baden. I was baptized there when I was about ten, went to confirmation class there and became a member after going through a catechism page by page with the minister. The Methodist Church did not believe in drinking alcohol. Apparently, when Jesus changed water into wine at the wedding in Cana, the Methodist Bible thought that the gospel author, John, must have meant grape juice. My mom insisted that we take church and the Bible seriously. As you will see, this had unintended consequences later. The other Protestant church in town was the Zion United Church of Christ (UCC). I'm not sure what the theological differences were between the Methodist and UCC churches. If there were any, maybe the UCC was more tolerant of alcohol.

St. George, the Catholic Church, was by far the biggest in New Baden. It had its own elementary school, its own cemetery and a church bell that chimed on the hour. The Germans who attended St. George did not seem to have the same aversion to alcohol that we Methodists had. I had little interaction with the Catholics—or "fish eaters," as we crudely called them—who attended the St. George School. (Those of us who attended the public school were "publics.")

After elementary school, most St. George kids attended the county Catholic High School, Mater Dei in Breese, about fifteen miles from New Baden. It occurs to me now that the parents of the small number of Catholic kids who went to Wesclin for high school probably couldn't afford the Mater Dei tuition.

During senior high, I became the president of the Methodist Youth Fellowship. By then, the New Baden and Trenton Methodist churches had a young minister, Carl Carter, who was more open-minded. During one discussion group, he asked us if only Christians went to heaven.

One boy, a couple years older, said he thought of heaven as having different gates for different beliefs. That wise comment has stayed with me.

In ninth grade, the sponsor of the National Junior Honor Society, Harriet Thomas, suggested that Junior Honor Society members from the

11

area should get together. We planned a meeting at Wesclin, sent out invitations to several schools and about five schools responded. One was an all-Black school from East St. Louis. For me, it was a very important event. I saw firsthand that being a different race did not mean the students were not smart or did not have the same aspirations I did, although I certainly did not understand all the obstacles they would face in achieving those aspirations.

I imagine that there were people in New Baden who saw young Black students get off the bus and head inside the junior high building and thought the world was ending. That was because New Baden was all White and not about to change. Just as the Methodist Church did not like alcohol, it did not like "colored people." According to one website, New Baden was quite possibly a "sundown town," meaning Black people had to be out of town by 5pm.[6] That seems perfectly plausible to me. To give a flavor of New Baden's culture, when I was in a grade school Sunday school class, the teachers organized us kids into a minstrel show. We wore blackface and learned Stephen Foster songs like "Old Black Joe" and performed around town. Not to be outdone, another Sunday school teacher told our junior high class that she did not want "colored people" moving to New Baden. It wasn't because she disliked them, she claimed. Instead, it was because it would lower property values. I could never understand how a Christian Sunday school teacher could voice an opinion so at odds with what the Bible taught. This was not the last time I faced this contradiction, and unfortunately it continues to this day.

By the time I reached high school, I had to ride a bus five miles to Trenton, and the bus seemed to take forever as it went down country roads to pick up kids who lived on farms. There were about 150 students in the school, and my senior class had 49, about 30 of whom were boys. I thought

---

6 https://sundown.tougaloo.edu/sundowntownsshow.php?state=IL

many of my classmates weren't smart, which was very short-sighted of me. My mother took pains to remind me frequently that "you think you're so smart," which she did not mean as a compliment. One of my classmates who did not do well in school ended up as a bank president.

I sometimes see Facebook posts about high school being the best years of some people's lives. Not me. Even after living in New Baden seven years, I still felt like an outsider. As a teacher's kid, both students and teachers either resented me or expected a lot from me.

I was disappointed in many of my high school teachers as well as some of my classmates. My high school history teacher, also the basketball coach, said in a class, "I never met a n----r who couldn't sing, dance or play ball." Plus, about the second week of sophomore year, I realized all he was doing was reading from the textbook. And our high school biology teacher told our class, on the eve of a field trip to the Climatron in St. Louis, "When you go through East St. Louis, don't make fun of the darkies." Her primary accomplishment in life had been to illustrate, many years earlier, a book called *Just Weeds*. Every year, she made her biology classes collect at least twenty samples of weeds, label them and present in a scrapbook. I took biology as a sophomore. One of the boys in the class, Clarence, was a senior, a very big guy and a chronic underachiever, who was a bully. He told me he had to pass this class to graduate and he wanted me to do his weed project for him. Of course, I was a little scared, but I figured it would not be too big of a deal, because if I was collecting weeds for myself, it would be easy to pick two of everything I collected. Plus, I thought it would be a way to get back at a teacher I did not like on an assignment I thought was stupid, and at which she expected Clarence to fail. So I did it; he received an A on the project and the rest of that year he made sure nothing happened to me.

High school summers I had my first job: I sold Fuller Brush products door to door. I walked the streets of New Baden, climbed the porch steps of houses where people I did not know lived and knocked on the door or rang the bell. If the lady of the house invited me in, I would go through the sales pitch I had been provided by the regional sales manager. I carried a suitcase filled with Fulsol degreaser, furniture polish and a variety of other cleaning products. I demonstrated them all and passed out pastry brushes or vegetable brushes as a free gift. I sometimes felt guilty when the house-wives or widows—practically every house in New Baden had a housewife or widow—bought things I was sure they could not afford, because I was confident our family could not afford them. I believe this experience made me never want to sell anything again.

By the spring of 1967, I was in my last high school semester, put-ting in my time until graduation, playing on the tennis and golf teams. One highlight of my senior spring was playing Jimmy Connors in tennis. He played for Assumption High School, a Catholic high school in East St. Louis, which later became a juvenile detention center surrounded by barbed wire as East St. Louis deteriorated. As a freshman, he was already getting national press, and I could see why. Every ball he hit went either just over the net or into the tape at the top of the net. He won 10-0, but my brother said it was the best match I ever played.

I also was playing organ in a garage band. (I bought the Farfisa minicompact with my Fuller Brush earnings.) Over the summer, I met an older guy whose brother had a band and he wanted to start a band. We got together with a drummer from the high school in an upstairs room in Trenton, to see what we could do. We started with "Gloria" but the sum-mer ended before we managed to learn many songs. Then, school and fall baseball intruded, and that was the end of my first band. During the school year, five or six students decided to form a band. None of us really could play our instruments, but we were enthusiastic. We even played for a junior high dance.

In class, however, I was bored. For example, in a chemistry class, the teacher was probably around fifty or sixty, unmarried, very bright and somewhat absentminded. One afternoon, I brought a tennis ball to class and when she turned her back to the class to write on the blackboard, I bounced the tennis ball off the blackboard she was writing on. She never noticed.

CHAPTER 2

NAVIGATING THE DRAFT

My goal was college, but there was an obstacle for all young men approaching high school graduation in 1967: the draft. In this era, once you graduated from high school, your future was determined by the draft and the Vietnam War. There was a complicated system of deferments for college and for certain other matters. 1-A, you were available for service; II-S, college student deferment; 1-S, high school student deferment; II-C, working in agriculture; II-D, studying to be a minister; 1-O, conscientious objector available for civilian service in the national interest; 1-OA, conscientious objector available for noncombat military service; 4-F, physically unqualified for service. There were probably a dozen other classifications. If you were male and had turned eighteen, you had one. Therefore, the war affected just about every American family.

While the draft had been in effect since World War II, by 1967 it was fearsome because the Vietnam War was expanding. For young men, there were only a few options: enlist; wait to get the letter that started "Greetings," telling you that you had been drafted; get a deferment, either for college attendance or for hardship; fail the draft physical and get a 4F classification; or apply for conscientious objector status. The easiest deferment was to go to college right after graduation. Several of my classmates planned to go to junior college; one was accepted at Northwestern University. Some talked of enlisting rather than waiting around to get drafted. You see, if you enlisted, you could select your branch of service (Army, Air Force, Navy, Marines, or Coast Guard), but you had to serve three years. If you were drafted, you went into the Army, but you only had to serve two years—but those two years might well include one in Vietnam. A few lived on farms and would probably be able to get an agricultural deferment. Another went to Canada. For others, it was the wait for the draft. These were hard choices for eighteen-year-olds, especially when politicians supported the war as necessary to defeat "communism." But Vietnam was a war with battles but no battlefronts, and it was far from certain that the United States was winning the war.

My plan was to get a student deferment and worry about the draft when I graduated. However, I was worried about how my parents would pay for college. In addition to my two brothers, by now I had a sister twelve years younger. My father, as a small-town junior high school teacher, barely made enough to support a family of six, and my mother did not work outside the home. I had no wealthy grandparents or aunts or uncles I could count on to help pay for my college education.

Fortunately, I was an exceptional student, and I was particularly good at taking standardized tests. As a junior, I scored well enough on the National Merit Scholarship test to be a finalist, the first at Wesclin. I was quickly accepted at the University of Illinois. In the back of my mind, I thought I might sign up for the Reserve Officers' Training Corps (ROTC), because you received some financial benefits. Then, I started receiving letters from colleges all over the country. It never occurred to me that with my grades and test scores, I might be able to get a full ride at an Ivy League school or some similar university. Instead, my alternative to the University of Illinois was West Point. West Point was highly rated, and it had the advantages of being far from New Baden and not costing my parents very much. Even now, US News and World Report ranks it number 18 among liberal arts colleges (for what that is worth), but in 1967, an appointment to West Point carried a lot of prestige.

Also, my parents had always encouraged me to consider West Point or the Air Force Academy. When I was about five, my mother spoke very highly of a young man in the small town we then lived in who had been accepted to the first Air Force Academy class.

There was an element of romance to West Point, which from the outside made it easy to overlook the nitty-gritty. Cadets in precise formation, the dignity of the gray stone buildings, following in the footsteps of legends like MacArthur and Eisenhower—it seemed like a pinnacle. In the documentary *No Direction Home*, Bob Dylan mentions that when he was eighteen and thinking about a college he would want to end up at, he considered West Point. It didn't happen, but just the fact that it crossed his mind shows the allure of the place to young, fearless and imaginative men (and now women).

Personally, I liked the idea of West Point because you had to compete to get in, and I was (and am) very competitive. (It did not occur to me that other universities were equally competitive, just not as obviously.) And going to West Point would solve the issue of how to deal with the draft beyond simply the college deferment. When you went to West Point, you became a member of the Army while in school, and after you graduated, you owed a minimum of five years of active duty, starting as a Second Lieutenant. In one sense, going to West Point deferred active duty, and like my father, I would be an officer. I felt that, with my abilities and my background, I could contribute more as an officer than as an enlisted man.

At West Point, you had to excel academically, but you also had to be in good physical condition, and your extra-curricular activities were supposed to play a part in getting admitted. I was involved in many activities: I lettered in four sports; I was in the high school band; I was in the Methodist Youth Fellowship; and I was a Lt. Colonel in the Civil Air Patrol. I had attended a mock United Nations at Southern Illinois University (where my roommate was the first Jewish person I had ever met—in New Baden, Jews were a rumor). In addition to my father and mother, my guidance counselors encouraged me to apply. I wrote letters to our congressman and senators, and I eventually received a slot as a third or fourth alternate. My chances seemed very slim. In the meantime, I qualified for various scholarships to lessen the financial burden on my parents if I went to U of I.

I was in French class in April 1967, enduring my last couple months of high school, when the principal, Donald Wherle, came into the class and said I had a phone call. This was unheard of. I walked up the stairs, into his office, and picked up the phone. It was the admissions office at West Point, telling me the school was offering me admission to the class of 1971. The person explained that the class entering West Point in July 1967 was expanding beyond the Congressional appointments due to the Vietnam War, and I was a "qualified alternate." It wasn't a difficult decision for me. I said yes.

The rest of the school year flew by. I went on the senior class bus trip to New York City and Washington, D.C. In New York City, my friends and I visited Greenwich Village, where the Lovin' Spoonful had written and recorded their first album. I walked down the stairs to the street from the top floor of the Empire State Building with my friend Hadley, who had been accepted to Northwestern. Hadley tragically died five years later from a heart attack. In June, the Beatles released *Sgt. Pepper's Lonely Hearts Club Band*. I was mesmerized by the album.

Then my life changed.

CHAPTER 3:

WHERE WAS VIETNAM AND WHY WERE WE IN A WAR THERE?

By the end of 1966, the United States had nearly 400,000 soldiers in Vietnam, and over 5,000 had been killed. While protests against the war were beginning in some colleges and cities, the majority of Americans still supported it, albeit reluctantly, because Vietnam was portrayed as the first of a series of dominoes that would inevitably fall to the "communists" if the US did not stand its ground there. That was the story President Johnson offered the country, and that was the consensus of most members of Congress. In the 1960s, and actually going back to President Eisenhower, the domino theory was an accepted part of American popular political culture. If Vietnam fell, then Laos would fall, then Cambodia, then Thailand and Malaysia, and before long there would be nothing but communists from the Soviet Union across Asia to Red China and Southeast Asia, and would Hawaii even be safe? The few senators who disagreed that the war was a vital national bulwark against the red menace were considered weak on communism. Of course, it sounds absurd now—or does it, given our country's twenty-year morass in Afghanistan and Iraq? But in the 1960s, keeping the United States free from communism was a cornerstone of American foreign policy. This was particularly true in little New Baden.

21

The war was on the network news every night, and in the 1960s, the evening network news was the way many people got their information. It got to the point where Walter Cronkite on *CBS* or Chet Huntley and David Brinkley on *NBC* would report, almost every night, the number of Americans and Vietnamese killed that day, a kind of perverse scorekeeping—we felt better if the Viet Cong and North Vietnamese body count was higher than that of the United States. Of course, we know now that the military gave the press bogus numbers and the military's preoccupation with body count incentivized officials to include women, children and noncombatants as part of the figures. Robert McNamara admitted as much in a 1967 memorandum to President Johnson that was released as part of the Pentagon Papers: the number of weapons the military recovered was only one-sixth the number of enemy troops reported as killed, suggesting the count included a large number of non-combatants. Secretary of Defense McNamara came up with the body count as a data-driven way of analyzing whether the war was successful. Generals Westmoreland and Abrams, who between them commanded United States forces in Vietnam from 1964 through 1972, were all too ready to latch on to this as an analytic they could use to further their careers, as Ken Burns' series on the Vietnam War made clear. The Pentagon Papers revealed that military decisions were being driven not just by the body count but also by other manipulated metrics, like expected replacement guerillas for those allegedly killed, tons of materiel North Vietnam was using in the war effort, tons of materiel being imported from the USSR and China, desertion reports, kill ratios and an endless list of statistics that were frequently updated to show the US getting the better of the North Vietnamese. The US was winning the Vietnam War and there was an end in sight; that was the public picture when I entered West Point.

Being admitted to West Point was a *big deal* to my family and in my small town. Of course, I was proud of having accomplished what had seemed like an improbable if not impossible goal. I basked in the attention until the time drew near for me to enroll, when I became scared to death. What had I got myself into? It wasn't the war that scared me—that was four years off, and I would be prepared, I was sure. What scared me was the two months of "Beast Barracks," and the entire plebe year.

On July 1, 1967, my family drove me to Lambert Airport in St. Louis, where I was torn between reluctance to leave my family and an adventure I wanted to get started. I guess I have always been impatient. At the airport, I ran into a member of a local band I followed called the Unknowns. It was kind of shocking to see him in the airport with a wife and a baby. It had not occurred to me that the people in the bands I would go see would have lives off the stage. It is an example of how naïve I was when I entered West Point.

I flew from Lambert to LaGuardia in New York City. I was seventeen. I have no idea where I stayed that night, but it might have been the same hotel we stayed on our senior class trip, which was toward Midtown. On my return, I ventured out on the subway to Greenwich Village like we had on the school trip, to a club called the Bitter End, and listened to a young singer with long, straight blonde hair named Joni Mitchell play with open tuning and sing about seagulls and a night in the city.

The next day, I followed the directions I had been sent to go to the Port Authority Bus Terminal, a noisy, crowded and mammoth building on Manhattan's west side. I, along with other nervous young men, found the right bus, and it drove us up Highway 9W to West Point, a ride that took about an hour and a half but covered only fifty-three miles because of the stops at towns on the way. Once there, I stayed that night at the Thayer Hotel, just inside the south gate.

It was the first glimpse of my scenic and historic home for the next three years.

—

West Point is set on the west bank of the Hudson River as it flows south past majestic Storm King Mountain, then drifts around Trophy Point and the gray stone walls of the academy. A few miles past West Point, the river passes under Bear Mountain Bridge, then travels on its way to New York Harbor and the Atlantic Ocean about sixty-five miles south.

When I stepped off the bus in 1967, just inside the gate, I could feel history. I'm sure newly arrived cadets still do. It is hard to overestimate the importance of West Point to the military history of our country; it is the oldest continuously occupied military post in America.

West Point's role in our nation's history started during the Revolutionary War. General George Washington considered it to be the most important strategic position in America due to its commanding position on the Hudson River. Washington personally selected Thaddeus Kosciuszko, the Polish Colonel who was assisting the revolutionary army, to design the fortifications for West Point in 1778, and General Washington transferred his headquarters there in 1779.

In 1780, General Benedict Arnold, who then was the commander at West Point, hatched a plot to surrender it to the British. Arnold's plot was foiled, and West Point was never captured by the British, despite Arnold's efforts. Rather, the name Benedict Arnold became a synonym for treason.

After the Revolutionary War, early American leaders, including General Washington, Alexander Hamilton and John Adams, urged the creation of a military academy to lessen the need for the new country to rely on foreign officers. In 1802, President Thomas Jefferson signed legislation establishing the United States Military Academy at West Point, after ensuring that those attending the academy would represent the citizens of a democratic society.

West Point is actually a 16,000-acre army base. Along with about 4,300 cadets, it has 1,200 active-duty soldiers and over 2,000 of their family members, and about 5,000 civilian personnel working there. The West Point campus, to the extent you could call the cadet portion of the army base a campus, surely rivals any in the country for pure beauty. Looking over Trophy Point north toward the steep bluffs of Storm King Mountain and the Hudson, it is as if you can see the "Vulture," the sloop Benedict Arnold and British Major Andre used during their treasonous plot, floating near the western banks of the river. Turn your eyes up and to the left, and you see the austere gothic Protestant Chapel standing guard. Behind you see the parade ground, where on fall and spring Saturday mornings you can watch cadets march in precise formation, not knowing the sotto voce conversation in the ranks: "Plebe, what's this march?" "What's the movie tonight?" "You better get in step, crot."

Up past the chapel was Michie Field, where Glenn Davis and Doc Blanchard played when Army football was among the best in the country, before college football became big business. Even in 1968, Army went 8-2 and was invited to the Sugar Bowl but turned down the invite due to tradition. Cadets were irate, and sugar bowls disappeared from the mess hall for a meal. That type of response also was tradition—the Long Gray Line.

On July 3, nervous and scared, I stepped into that tradition. Putting on a brave front, I walked the mile or so from the hotel to a gym, along with other young men, all of us acting as if this was just another field trip. Somehow, we all ended up in a locker room, where everyone was given shorts, tee shirts, socks, and shoes, told to dress and to report to the man in the red sash. I began to relax. This wasn't so bad. An innocent-looking young man led us out of the gym single file toward a destination that looked about half a mile away. There was a noise in the distance that got louder with each step.

Soon, we were in line before an arched entryway, which we came to know as a sally port, facing the man in the red sash. The noise we had been hearing, which we now recognized as chaotic yelling, was deafening from inside the sally port—then intimidating. This was the beginning of New Cadet Barracks, or Beast Barracks, as it is commonly known.

Beast Barracks is the two-month summer training regime where new cadets are plunged into harsh mental and physical pressure and military discipline. The goal is to immediately teach them that in the military, discipline is king, so that they learn the unquestioning obedience they will one day expect from the soldiers they lead. Coping with this constant pressure removes much of a new cadet's individual personality in favor of the morale and success of the unit.

I stood before the man in the red sash, terrified. He was young but imposing, a wall of authority. He wore gray pants, a white shirt with epaulets and a service hat, with a ruby red sash diagonally across his shirt and around his waist. I could see into a concrete square with a yellowish clock tower in the center enclosed by three-story brick buildings I soon learned were barracks. Young men were running back and forth in white tee shirts and gray gym shorts, most with extreme buzz cuts, with more men dressed like the man in front of us, minus the sash, yelling and directing. It was bewildering, chaotic. I suspect it is similar today, except that there are women wearing the red sash too.

"Drop your bags!" the man yelled at me. "Pick them up! Drop them! Pick them up!" Eventually, after I was told repeatedly that I was lower than a worm, I was sent to the barbershop in the basement at the corner of the enclosed square, where I was quickly scalped, like all the other new cadets. This square, known as the Central Area, was surrounded on three sides with yellow brick barracks with a porch running in front and periodic steps up to the porch. The fourth side was an imposing dark gray stone barracks. A clock tower stood in the middle of the Central Area. We had to double-time (run)[7] outside the barracks and square corners when we changed direction, which meant that each turn we made had to be ninety degrees. No cutting corners! One of the young men in charge taught me to brace, a physical position new cadets were required to assume everywhere except in our rooms, during physical training or in the field. Bracing meant standing at ramrod attention, with your head and eyes forward, chin in, your shoulders back and your chest up. Plebes also had to maintain this posture at meals, which we ate slowly, one bite at a time. Bracing was both physically uncomfortable and mentally stressful because you never knew who was watching. It was a constant reminder you had no inherent value.

I frankly don't recall much else about the rest of the day, except there were hours of close-order drill, which involved training new cadets in the marching commands and movements needed for the parade for the parents. This was one area where I was ready because I had learned close-order drill in the Civil Air Patrol and had marched in parades in high school band, although not with my chin pressed into my neck. I will hand it to the cadet leaders: that first day, July 3, 1967, they managed to whip 1,200 terrified and bewildered young men, all high-achievers before that day, into a semblance of a military marching unit that circled the parade ground in front of proud parents who would not see their sons for months and who for the most part had no idea what they were about to face. The high point of the parade and ceremony was when the plebes took their oath:

---

7 "Double-time" in the military officially means marching at a pace of 180 steps per minute. Informally, it means running.

> I, Cary Donham, do solemnly swear that I will support
> the Constitution of the United States, and bear true alle-
> giance to the National Government; that I will maintain
> and defend the sovereignty of the United States, para-
> mount to any and all allegiance, sovereignty, or fealty I
> may owe to any State or Country whatsoever; and I will at
> all times obey the legal orders of my superior officers and
> the Uniform Code of Military Justice.

I am certain that I, like all other plebes, meant these words whole-heartedly. I still do. I also believe that despite the way my path would later change, my actions always were consistent with them.

At the end of the day, we were assigned to a room in what was then known as East Barracks. There were three beds, two being a bunk. On each bed there was a jumble of clothes, toiletries, paper, and pens littered about. I met my first two roommates, Scott Crandall from Iowa and Ron Cleary from South Carolina. We were "introduced" to our squad leaders, "Mr. Ennis, Sir!" and "Mr. Belack, Sir!" Belack had posters in his room of the Israeli army, which had just crushed Egypt in the Six-Day War. Ennis was generally a good guy, demanding but fair, but he had a job to do: turn three civilian men used to being hot shots into young men able to withstand the rigors of West Point life. My roommates and I were exhausted that first day, wondering when things would calm down. Sorry, boys, not for a long time.

West Point had assigned us and about 140 other plebes to Second Company, 1 of 8 new cadet companies. First and Second Company cadet officers and squad leaders came from the First Regiment, Third and Fourth Company cadet officers and squad leaders came from the Second Regiment and so on through the Fourth Regiment. West Point and its tradition intended for Beast Barracks to be mentally and emotionally demanding. However, it was especially brutal in the First Regiment companies because the First Regiment had the reputation, well deserved, of having the strictest discipline toward plebes—or, as we were called in harsher moments, crots or smackheads or beanheads. ("Beanhead" referred to the omnipresent buzz cuts all new cadets were required to sport, and I have always assumed that smack involved an implicit warning— "Shape up or I will smack you in the head." But I never knew exactly where "crot" came from except it was really bad.)

I wrote to my parents about that first day: "Monday was the hardest day. We spent most of the day drilling to get ready for the ceremony at Trophy Point. (I'm now in the army). . . . The three meals are the worst part of the day. Most of the stuff has been issued to us by now, but it's not put away yet. I've got to get everything ready by Saturday, but I don't know how or when. We don't have time to do anything. Next week the real training starts so things won't be getting any better. It's going to be a long hard year."

CHAPTER 4:

BEAST BARRACKS

There was a lot to absorb in a very short time. We had to learn what the different uniforms were and how to wear them. We had to get used to the Hellcats drum and bugle corps blowing reveille at 6am to jar us from the little sleep we were allowed. We had to learn to get dressed quickly, get outside for breakfast formation and find our correct places. We had to learn that we were constantly being observed. And we had to learn we were powerless. The only escape was to resign—which, over the first few weeks, a number of plebes did. The thought crossed my mind, as it crossed the minds of many new cadets. New cadets were universally struggling, some mentally, some physically, some both—but there was support in this shared struggle. We had worked hard to get here, and for most new cadets, including me, admitting you couldn't hack it was not an option.

In addition to getting used to the constant pressure and the new routine, during our first ten days at West Point, we had a class in tent pitching, conditioning exercises and a two-hour conditioning march. I wrote to my parents, "It wasn't real easy, but when we got to the camp, we stayed overnight Tuesday night, and got to eat two meals there. We didn't have to brace for either one, which made the whole thing worthwhile." We were constantly changing uniforms. Back from the march at the Academy grounds, we left behind our fatigues for khakis for a lecture on the Honor Code. We changed into a uniform called "sierra" for supper, which was gray trousers and white shirts with epaulettes, then back to fatigues after supper.

It must have been a tough week, because I later wrote:

> It is now Saturday afternoon. We had the inspection this morning, in the rooms and in the ranks without rifles. I could have done better. Yesterday was a hard day. There were conditioning exercises, drill, a class on taking apart the rifle, a class on movements of the infantry soldier and several other classes. In addition, I had to stay up till about 1:00am working on the room. . . . This is the easiest place in the world to get discouraged. These last weeks, when I look back, have gone fast, but it still seems like I've been here a year. It really isn't anything like I thought it would be. The worst part is the pressure—to change uniforms in five minutes for the next formation—to get your room spotless and to always look perfect because if you don't you'll hear about it. I don't feel like quitting, or I'm not even considering it but sometimes, like right now, I regret having come. Don't get worried now. I'm all right. It's just that it's easy to get down in this place and hard to get up. You can't stay down long, though, because there is always something for you to prepare for and always something to look forward to.

By the second week of Beast Barracks, the constant pressure was taking a toll on most plebes' morale. Little did we know that West Point officers shared our observation about pressure being the most difficult aspect so far. Unknown to us, some officers were beginning to question, at least internally, whether Beast Barracks was the best way to teach discipline and leadership. I located an internal study prepared in 1968–1969 by a group of officers who were charged with studying the pros and cons of the "Fourth Class System," the overall environment plebes faced during their first year at West Point. These officers justified hazing by concluding that "the Fourth Class System is an artificially generated stressful situation which facilitates the socialization and equalization of cadets, assists in the identification: 'it is stress.'"[8]

Stress predominated from the second I heard the roar coming from Central Area. Stress was constant, partly because discipline was often arbitrary. I could be corrected anytime, anyplace, for anything, real, imagined or contrived. There was stress to make each formation in the correct uniform, on time, in the right spot, with shoes shined and belt buckle polished. There was even more stress if one of my weekly duties for the company was to give the countdown to reveille formation, or lunch formation, or a parade, or dinner formation: standing at the end of a hall, plebes in every barracks, for each of the eight companies, in a brace, yelling at the top of their lungs, "There are fifteen minutes to breakfast formation! Uniform for breakfast formation is fatigues! Fifteen minutes, sir!" Then the same for ten minutes, five minutes, four, three, two, one minute, at which point the hapless plebe might have to dash down three flights of stairs, run to the formation and get in place, again at attention and bracing, before the entire corps was called to attention.

There was rarely enough time to breathe between events, and our lives were generally scheduled down to the minute from 6am to 10pm daily. There also was the stress of memorizing information such as the menu and the weekly movies, as well as pieces plebes had to learn verbatim from *Bugle Notes*, often called the Plebes' Bible, which ranged from a few lines

---

8 "A Preliminary Evaluation of the Fourth Class System" 1969, 5.

to several paragraphs. Sometimes an upperclassman would request longer pieces, especially if he had a plebe on the defensive. "Donham, smack; let's hear Battalion Orders!" At which point I would be expected to recite:

> But an officer on duty knows no one—to be partial is to dishonor both himself and the object of his ill-advised favor. What will be thought of him who exacts from his friends that which disgraces him! Look at him who winks at and overlooks offenses in one, which he causes to be punished in another, and contrast him with the inflexible soldier who does his duty faithfully, notwithstanding it occasionally wars with his private feelings. The conduct of one will be venerated and emulated, the other detested as a satire upon soldiership and honor.

If I survived that, and the upperclassman was really pissed off, he might say, "Okay, let's hear Schofield's Definition of Discipline." I would then be expected to spout:

> The discipline which makes the soldiers of a free country reliable in battle is not to be gained by harsh or tyrannical treatment. On the contrary, such treatment is far more likely to destroy than to make an army.

At that point, I would silently ask myself whether he even heard what I was reciting, since it seemed contrary to his harsh and tyrannical treatment of me, while at the same time trying to continue:

> It is possible to impart instruction and to give commands in such a manner and in such a tone of voice to inspire in the soldier no feeling but an intense desire to obey, while the opposite manner and tone of voice cannot fail to excite

strong resentment and a desire to disobey. The one mode or the other of dealing with subordinates springs from a corresponding spirit in the breast of the commander. He who feels the respect which is due to others cannot fail to inspire in them regard for himself, while he who feels and thence manifests, disrespect toward others, especially his inferiors, cannot fail to inspire hatred against himself.

I wondered whether the upperclassmen understood the irony of making plebes recite this passage, taken from an 1879 address to the Corps of Cadets, when they had no incentive to inspire respect from plebes; they could obtain obedience through bullying. Of course, too often they themselves had been bullied as plebes, especially in the First Regiment, which viewed plebe hazing as tradition, if not a blood sport. I suspect that the enthusiasm with which upperclassmen in the classes of 1968 and 1969 ran roughshod over plebes ill prepared them for leading the drafted citizen-soldiers compelled to fight in Vietnam.

Looking back, the second week was perhaps more difficult than the first. We had an inspection and I, like most new cadets, received demerits. You could get up to fifteen before you were disciplined—which meant hours on a Saturday afternoon, during privilege time, walking across the Central Area in full dress uniform carrying your rifle on your shoulder as the seconds crawled by. It was painful, physically and mentally. At least that second week, I escaped walking the area. I wrote:

In some ways, the weekends are rougher than the weeks right now, because you have time to think. During the week, you don't have time to think, or do anything but what they tell you, two weeks ago today I was a civilian, wondering what this place would be like. Now I know. It

35

seems so long ago I could do what I wanted. These restrictions aren't easy to adjust to. I just wish I could describe my life here, but I can't. You have to live here before you can understand what somebody means by: Beast Barracks." You can't do anything right, but if you don't, you get yelled at. Almost everywhere you have to brace. Maybe next Saturday at privileges things will look better, but sometimes this place seems pointless— small bites, bracing, no sleep, memorizing, running up all stairs. I can do it but sometimes I wish I would have taken the easy way out and gone to U of I. . . . Next week will probably be rough: there are no marches, but there is a three-hour class in tactics on Tuesday morning, which will probably include a half-mile doubletime with rifles at port arms just to get there. Next Saturday there is a parade, so we will be doing a lot of drill this week. Probably before I know, Saturday will be here, but it seems a long way off.

It turns out my prediction was wrong in one way: we went to the tactics class in trucks, and while there, we were allowed to eat without bracing. Eating was an obsession, because plebes were often hungry and tired, so a full meal was a *big deal*. Here is how I described the three-hour class to my folks:

All morning was a tactics class . . . The classes were on field fortifications. Camouflage, throwing hand grenades and an obstacle course. The obstacle course wasn't the kind you think of. It had 5 obstacles (1) a ditch to go through (2) barbed wire to go under (3) a low log fence to roll over (4) more barbed wire (5) a wall chest high to go over. We had to crawl through the course, about 25 or

30 yards between obstacles. Part of the course was muddy, and everyone was filthy but happy because we got to eat. However, the boots and my rifle were dirty. . . I suppose you are wondering when I have time to write this letter. The answer: right now it is about 11:15pm. I'm sitting in bed, using the light from the hall. Tomorrow night is chapel—everyone will get a coke. The rest of the week will be hard, but I can make it.

Reading this letter, from July 18, 1967, is a bit of a surprise, because I remember that wall looking twenty feet high.

I already spoke of stress at meal times. There were other tasks where, due to varying backgrounds, different plebes felt different levels of trauma. For me, trying to qualify at the rifle range was high stress. For some, it was a piece of cake. I had never fired any type of weapon before arriving at West Point. The only weapon I had even handled was a pistol that didn't work—my grandma Myrtle kept it under her bed because she thought it might scare a burglar.

Now I was given an M-14 semi-automatic rifle.

We kept these in our rooms and used them mostly in parades. But we had to learn to take them apart, clean them and fire them to qualify as a marksman by hitting about half the targets in a timed segment. We had a couple of hours of instruction and practice on the range and then we had the qualification round. The range had lanes about 350 yards long. Targets—each the torso and head of a person—would pop up in the lane for a couple of seconds, and I had to locate the target, fire and hit it before it disappeared. The one thing I remember about qualifying was that I had to pee really badly, but I was afraid to ask the soldier who was teaching me if there was somewhere I could go. As with any task, having to pee really badly makes one squirm. There is nothing worse if you are trying to lay still and site a target 200 yards away quickly, and slowly squeeze the trigger. If I failed, first, there would be humiliation; second, there would be additional instructions away from the squad, and I would have to make up the items I missed. In the end, I hit exactly 50% and, more importantly at the time, made it to a portable bathroom without wetting my fatigues. On the other hand, plebes who had grown up hunting qualified easily.

Training marches, or long hikes, were another part of Beast Barracks. They were stressful for some new cadets, but not for me. I had good endurance and could easily go ten miles with a pack and rifle, and hiking up the ski slope was not a problem. The squad leaders would try to keep spirits up by leading chants, known as Jody cadences.

Leader: "I don't know, but I've been told, Company 2 is good as gold. Sound off!"

Squad: "One, two!"

Leader: "Say it again!"

Squad: "Three, four! One, two, three, four! One, two, three, four!"

There were other cadences that bordered on the obscene—"I know a girl all dressed in black, she makes her living on her back," and so on. Almost anything to pass the time on a grueling ten-mile hike in the middle of summer. Most of us did fine on the hikes, but occasionally there was a straggler. He could be developing a blister, or becoming fatigued. Squad leaders would treat a blister as best as they could and encourage a straggler to push on, but make no mistake: stragglers were remembered.

I don't remember what actually happened once we arrived where we were going on those marches. What mattered to me was the food and that plebes were treated like new soldiers being trained, not like, well, crots, or smacks, or some other variety of scum. We were allowed to eat freely in the field. Mess trucks would meet the company at some destination, and everyone could eat without bracing. There were only three or four marches during Beast Barracks, but they were the one time when the playing field between upper class and plebes was leveled a bit.

Marches back were filled with a gathering sense of dread as we got closer and closer to the Central Area barracks. Back to bracing, to being hyperalert upon stepping outside your room so you could slam against a wall if an upperclassman passed, to hurriedly writing down menus from bulletin boards, to shining shoes to a mirror-like surface and belt buckles to a high sheen. In short, back to incessant pressure.

About the third Saturday afternoon, plebes were allowed to make phone calls. There were lines at the phones. When I called home, collect, and my parents answered, I couldn't talk for a few seconds—I was on the verge of tears. How could I explain Beast Barracks to them when I was seventeen and in the middle of it? I am sure that my experience was similar to that of most plebes. Some plebes called girlfriends who, if they did not live in the New York-New JerseyConnecticut area, would not be seen until the Army-Navy game in Philadelphia at the earliest, or more likely at Christmas. By that time, the boys they had kissed goodbye on July 2 would be unalterably changed, physically and emotionally, in ways those outside could not imagine. What we did not consider was that the young women entering college would be changing too, and that in the general atmosphere of 1967, the changes cadets were going through would not universally be regarded as positive.

That same Saturday, we were allowed to buy snacks at the Boodler's, which was a small shop on the stoop level of the Central Area barracks, near the sally port where we had first met the man with the red sash. There also was a line at the Boodler's because we were *hungry*. Some upperclassmen encouraged us to take advantage of the brief opportunity to stuff ourselves, and we inhaled cookies, ice cream, Twinkies, and chips in stunning quantities. We of course expected that come dinner, we would be back to bracing, one bite at a time, looking straight ahead, expecting a reprimand, deserved or not, at any time.

Wrong again. The particularly ruthless heads of the dinner tables knew exactly what we had been doing all afternoon—stuffing ourselves like pigs. Imagine our surprise when we were encouraged to eat, to take big bites.

"Donham, don't you like the spaghetti and meatballs? They're my favorite. I consider it a personal insult that you're not eating up, and I know you don't want to get me angry, do you?"

"No, sir."

"Then eat up. Take big bites."

And so it went at most First Regiment Cadet Company tables. I know a couple of plebes in my company were sick that night. That's how it was that summer: learn and try to survive.

Plebes and upperclassmen as well, spent what seemed like an inordinate amount of time shining shoes. On the one hand, shined shoes do look good and, I suppose, can give a person a sense of pride in his (or her, now that females are admitted) appearance. On the other hand, to get a good spit-shine base can take hours, and it didn't come easy to me. What a way to spend precious free time: three seventeen- or eighteen-year-olds, who first met three weeks ago, sitting in a dorm room, each with a can of black Kiwi polish and cotton balls. Thankfully, a couple of men had attended the USMA Prep School in Ft. Belvoir, Virginia, and already knew what to do, which they passed on by word of mouth. Put on a thick layer of Kiwi, rub it in, dip the cotton ball in water and rub in circles. At first, it is just mud, but keep adding layers, rubbing it in and working with the cotton

40

ball. Eventually the toe and heels will emerge with a mirror-like finish. But this process could take a couple of hours, especially at first. Woe to those who waited until the last minute because the dull shine would betray your (relative) indolence.

Plebes could also get caught in a vicious circle. Perhaps I forgot an insecure upperclassman's beverage at dinner, and they took the offense personally. "My room after dinner, Donham, you useless smack."

After dinner, with fear and trembling, I would knock on the vengeful upperclassman's door: "New Cadet Donham, reporting as ordered, sir."

The door opens.

"Get in here, against the wall, Donham. Get than chin in. Is that the best you can do? I said get that chin in."

At this point, the upperclassman's head is literally inches from mine, and he is speaking loudly, as if I am outside the room, door closed, and down a flight of stairs.

"So it's not important to you to know I drink iced tea at dinner, smack? Are you stupid?"

"No, sir."

"You know you're supposed to know my beverage, don't you, Donham?"

"Yes, sir."

"So why did you send me a glass of water at dinner?"

"No excuse, sir."

"Let's see what else you don't know. What's for breakfast tomorrow?"

And so on, until the upperclassman lost interest in the game, like a dog might grow tired of gnawing a bone, and sent me packing back to my room.

Now I'm behind the eight ball. While I have been the chew toy of an upperclassman, my roommates have been getting their shoes and belt buckles ready for tomorrow morning's inspection. Perhaps my shoes aren't in such hot shape. In fifteen minutes, at 8pm, there is an evening class on etiquette, since West Point trains cadets to be officers *and* gentlemen. By the time we double-time back to the Central Area, it's 9:45pm, with lights out at 10:15pm. Just to make sure we knew, a bugler played taps every weekday night.

The next morning, my hastily shined shoes draw unwelcome attention from the company commander at inspection. Which leads to more hazing at lunch—not being allowed to eat, constantly being asked to recite more information, such as Battalion Orders. Only if I survive that onslaught will the upperclassman turn his attention to a different misstep by a different plebe.

But if an errant plebe continued to mess up, whether it is from nervousness, stress, fear or lack of time, a downward spiral could start. Upperclassmen could easily make a single plebe's life a living hell, having determined that the plebe just didn't have what it took to make it at West Point. The worst form of hazing was the clothing formation. The hapless plebe would be ordered outside the barracks in the appropriate uniform for the day. Then his upperclassman tormentor would order him to return to his room and return in a different uniform in five minutes, maybe full dress gray under a long overcoat, which includes the tall dress hat used in parades. Then, after the flaws in the hastily assembled uniform were carefully pointed out, with corresponding demerits, the upperclassman would send him back to his room to change to a different uniform in five minutes—maybe fatigues, which included combat boots, which by themselves could take minutes to put on and lace up. You get the idea. The victim's roommates would help, but there was only so much they could do.

Clothing formations were cruel. During Beast Barracks 1967, there were a number of plebes who simply threw in the towel, quit and returned home to the draft.

Fortunately, while I endured my share of hazing during Beast Barracks, I didn't stand out as either exceptionally gung-ho or exceptionally inept. It should be clear why I wouldn't want to become exceptionally inept because you wore a target on your forehead and back. However, being a military standout, which was open only to a few who seemed to have an innate feel for military life, was not much better. For example:

"Donham, is that the best you can do with your belt buckle? And your name tag is crooked. Take a look at New Cadet X sometime and maybe you can learn how a new cadet is supposed to look."

Meanwhile, New Cadet X is turning red and trying not to squirm because he has just raised the bar for his entire squad, a bar that had already seemed unattainable.

One appointment never changed during my three years, starting with my first week of Beast Barracks: Cadet Chapel. When I was at West Point, Chapel was mandatory. By regulation, Cadets were either Protestant, Catholic or Jewish: "Attendance at Chapel is part of a cadet's training; no cadet is exempt. Each cadet must attend either the Cadet Chapel, Catholic Chapel or Jewish Chapel service on each Sunday, according to announced schedules."[9] In other words, no Latter-Day Saints, no Buddhists and no practicing atheists on Sunday mornings. Each of these accepted religions had its cadet slang name: Catholics, mackerel snappers; Jews, ham dodgers; and Protestants, mountain climbers. While the first two were politically incorrect dietary references, the Protestant name referred to the fact that the Protestant Chapel was on a hill that rose above the barracks area.

---

9 Regulations for the United States Cadet Corps of the United States Military Academy, Chapter 8, Section IV, paragraph 819.

In 1970, two West Point cadets and nine midshipmen from the Naval Academy filed a class action lawsuit claiming that mandatory chapel violated the First Amendment. In the first legal go-round, in 1971, the federal district court ruled against the cadet plaintiffs. At least that judge entered an injunction against the military academies disciplining any of the cadets and midshipmen directly involved in the lawsuit. Then, in 1972, after I had left West Point, the United States Court of Appeals in the District of Columbia reversed that decision and threw out mandatory chapel because it interfered with cadets' free exercise of their religious rights and amounted to the establishment of a government-sponsored religion. The decision said that "this case does not involve programs vital to our immediate national security or even to military operational or disciplinary procedures.[10] I did not hear about this lawsuit while I was at West Point and I did not know the cadets who filed the lawsuit, but they each had to have had a pair of cojones to take on the Academy.

During Beast Barracks, Protestant Chapel was outside at Trophy Point, which has a magnificent view looking north down the Hudson River. Members of the Army band would play for the hymns and one of the three Protestant chaplains would conduct the service. It was peaceful, a contrast with the frenetic pace of the rest of the week. As I had grown up as a Methodist, attending church almost every Sunday, mandatory chapel did not seem like a huge burden, other than taking away a couple of hours that could have been spent sleeping on Sunday morning. But as time went on, the irony of a military chaplain telling would-be soldiers to love their neighbor and that soldiers had a high moral calling because they were called on to take other people's lives would begin to gnaw at me. But not that first summer. We had no time for such philosophical questions, internal debates, or quandaries. That all came later.

Halfway through Beast Barracks, the group of upperclassmen who were training plebes changed, and in early August, parents were invited to visit West Point and spend a few minutes with their sons. My parents came, but I was disappointed because once again I had to walk the area the Saturday afternoon when they were there. Still, I was glad to see them—but then it was back to my new reality. At that point, there were only a couple weeks to go in Beast Barracks. I don't recall anything about my second squad leaders, but apparently we did not get along because I wrote my parents that they "don't like me, for some reason, and they give me all kinds of trouble. We had a long hike this week and we have another Monday. We have drill, manual [of arms], bayonet, etc. all week long. I did pretty good in the inspection today, and I shouldn't have to walk next week. It's hard to believe that there are only two weeks until Beast Barracks is over and three weeks until classes start. I still don't like this very much but I guess I can make two more weeks." In the same letter, I also mentioned that during the plebe hike the last week, there would be a talent show, and some plebes from Second Company—including me—were somehow putting together a band to play at the talent show, using the equipment of an upperclassmen's band. So, while at this point I had 7/8 of my body and mind in the Army, I still was trying to keep a few toes in the real world.

Even though Beast Barracks was drawing to a close, the challenges were not. As I mentioned, we were given custody of an M14 rifle, along with a chrome dress bayonet for parades, a real bayonet and a rifle cleaning kit. Weight training was not common in 1967, and we developed upper-body strength through pushups, pull-ups and, during Beast Barracks, rifle exercises. Rifle exercises involved using your M14 like a weight, holding it in front of you, holding it over your head, holding it out while moving your arms side to side. It seemed like they always took place in the afternoon sun, too.

We also took part in bayonet drill, a part of Beast Barracks that made me uncomfortable. We were out in a large field away from the main parade ground, in uniforms consisting of gray shorts and tee shirts and combat boots, in rows with a squad leader on a platform in front of us. The squad leader would demonstrate moves with the bayonet and would yell, "What's the spirit of the bayonet, men?" We had to answer at the top of our lungs, "To kill, sir!" We would thrust forward our rifles with the bayonets fixed on the end, sweat dripping into our eyes. I went along, rationalizing that this was something I had to do to get through Beast Barracks and that fighting with a bayonet was a remnant of past wars. Little did I realize that in two years, I would be leading bayonet training—or how deeply it would affect me then.

During the next to last week on Monday morning, plebes had to go into a tear-gas-filled tent wearing gas masks, and then take them off while inside. I wrote to my folks, "It isn't hard to see how that stuff stops riots. Then, that afternoon we went on a four-hour conditioning march, including hiking up the ski slope. Tuesday was the obstacle course, bayonet drill, marching drill, manual of arms and other fun classes. And so on."

The last week of Beast Barracks featured the Plebe Hike to Lake Frederick. We left at 8am, walked until 11:15am, ate C rations and watched a demonstration by a rifle squad. After lunch, we marched the rest of the thirteen miles and arrived at Lake Frederick, where we pitched tents and went swimming. All in all, it was the least stressful day of Beast Barracks. Most notably, I learned to drive a deuce-and-half truck, and our makeshift band played at the talent show. I asked my parents to tell my brother that we played "Louie Louie" and "A Little Bit of Soul." I did not have to march back because I had aggravated a groin strain I had from the previous week and a doctor ordered me not to hike.

By August 28, 1967, Beast Barracks was over, and I had survived.

CHAPTER 5:

GETTING DOWN TO BUSINESS

The Army likes numbers that can be divided by two. When I started at West Point, there were eight New Cadet companies, with eight squads apiece of about sixteen new cadets. These eight New Cadet companies fed into the four regiments that comprised the Corps of Cadets, named—surprise—First Regiment, Second Regiment, Third Regiment and Fourth Regiment.

Each regiment was divided into eight companies, A through G; each company had, as best as I can remember, three platoons, and each platoon had four squads. There were about 120 cadets in each company.

As luck would have it, I ended up in Company F1, which I soon learned had the reputation for being one of the most enthusiastic (if not the most enthusiastic) proponents of and experts in plebe hazing in the Corps of Cadets. It was a source of pride, as well as competition with other First Regiment second battalion companies, and the 1967 version did its best to live up to that reputation. I can't remember all the first classmen who made making plebes' lives miserable their mission, but there were plenty. This lasted at least until late in the second semester, when first classmen were allowed to buy cars and leave the post more often.

The worst in Company F-1 was Jay Francis. He was ruthless when it came to plebe hazing; I suspect he had a reputation across the entire First Regiment, if not the entire Corps of Cadets. His favorite term for a plebe was "smack." Looking back and realizing he was only about twenty-one years old is startling, because at the time he was larger than life and to be avoided at all costs. The F-1 plebes had to do a Christmas skit for the upperclassmen, and we sang, to the tune of "Hey Joe," a then familiar song by the Byrds, Jimi Hendrix and a band called Love, "Hey Jay, where you going with that plebe in your hand?" to much merriment from plebes and upperclassmen. I do not believe Jay was a top-notch student, and he was likely headed for the infantry when he graduated. I don't know whether he was scared to death about his future as a second lieutenant in the infantry in Vietnam or was looking forward to killing Viet Cong. Maybe a little bit of both. I sure hope he did not treat the draftees in his infantry platoon like he treated plebes.

Reorganization Week is the week after the end of Beast Barracks and the beginning of the academic year. It was also a necessary pain in the ass. Everyone returns to the campus from leave or a summer assignment including plebes, exhausted from completing Beast Barracks. Everyone, including upperclassmen, had to get organized and obtain his room assignment and get his room ready. Then, we had to get books, and mainly to readjust to daily academy life. For plebes, it was even more hectic because we faced a new and unfamiliar daily grind. Sympathetic upperclassmen told us that the best thing for us to do would be to stay in our rooms as much as possible, and that is what I did.

The week was a blur. I had new roommates I had to get to know. Instead of two or three upperclassmen at mess hall tables, there were at least seven, and you had to learn all their beverage preferences. Table assignments changed every week or so, and you would find plebes huddled around the bulletin board writing down the upperclassmen at their tables. Now, unlike in Beast Barracks where a majority of people around me were scared plebes, Plebes were now a terrified minority, doing our best not to offend the upperclassmen we did not know: yearlings (sophomores), cows (juniors)[10] and firsties (seniors). Beast Barracks had been just a taste. Plebes still had a lot to learn and a short time to do it.

Reorganization Week was a hassle for everyone, not just plebes. Cadets had to roll in, figure out where their rooms were and find the stuff they had stored somewhere in one of the barracks basements. All cadets had to make sure their uniforms were presentable, and re-orient themselves to the day-to-day West Point life.

I still have recurring nightmares about Reorganization Week. They center on trying to recall where I stored my school-year uniforms while I was away for the summer. In these nightmares, I must get ready for a formation and I have no uniforms and no idea where they are. And in these nightmares, I'm not a plebe anymore, but it doesn't matter. I'm always late.

Company F1 was housed in what was then called Old South barracks, now known as Grant Barracks, on the south end of the Central Area, which were divided into three- or fourstory "divisions." There was a porch extending in front of the Old South barracks (called a stoop), and there were steps to the stoop with entry doors to the barracks divisions every fifty or sixty feet. Each door led to a four-story section of the barracks. Each company had four of these sections. The floor of one section had the company office, where mail was delivered, and two cadet rooms, while each other floor had four rooms. The rooms were not too different from

10 West Point legend suggests that juniors, as long ago as the 1840s, became known as cows because of weight they gained over the summer after yearling year due to the lousy food at the academy during the school year.

many college dorm rooms. Usually, there were three cadets to each, except for firsties and some cows.

Each cadet had a desk. There was a bunk bed and a second bed on the other side of the room. There was a closet for uniforms, with drawers for socks, underwear and tee shirts. Civilian clothes were not allowed. There also was a sink, and a rifle rack. There were rules as to how the uniforms were to be hung and how the drawers were to be set up. Woe to you during inspections if you did not pay attention to these rules.

I was relieved by the start of school because academics were something familiar. I wrote my parents:

> The academics aren't really that hard, except for math, but if you spend two hours a night on math, that leaves one hr. for two other subjects, plus shining shoes, straightening room, etc., so that you really have to work to get everything done. Add to this the fact that you are graded every day, and every day you come in the class, you might have a quiz, and you can see it's a little different from high school. You have to study here [unlike high school where I could pretty much skate by in second gear]. Really, there is probably more pressure now than ever before, but it's a different kind and everybody is under the same pressure. There is less hazing now, but there still is plenty . . . . Right now, West Point is a little more like I expected it.

Plebe year, there were no electives other than the foreign language you took. You had six hours of calculus, four hours of English, two and half hours of Engineering Fundamentals, military science, a foreign language (for me, French) and geography. Plus physical education.

50

Plus intramurals. Plus parades. Plus inspections. Plus keeping upper-classmen off your back. Other than that, it was just like college.

Calculus was central to plebe academics because it was important to the science and engineering classes that everyone would have to take as upperclassmen. Calculus was the first class of the day and lasted for an hour and twenty minutes, six days a week. The classes met in sections of about eighteen, with desks in a U shape surrounded by chalk boards. This was before calculators, so you had to take a slide rule to all math and science classes. There was an assignment every day. Every day, everyone in the class had to go to the board and work out a problem the instructor would assign, and you were graded on your public work. A few people were called on to explain their work. Heaven help a plebe who was not prepared. Not only would he get a very low grade for the day, there was the public humiliation. Of course, it happened to almost everyone at some point, except for the few who had studied calculus in high school or for whom math came naturally. I had not studied calculus in high school but I did grasp the basics pretty quickly, and after a while I went into an advanced section. There, the incentive was to work your ass off because you were competing with the plebes who had both studied calculus in high school (Dennis Winkler comes to mind) or had a knack for math (Mike Liberty, who later was my roommate). Fortunately, I did pretty well.

On the other hand, physical education was torture for me. At most colleges, physical education is not required, and if it is, it is a cupcake class. Not so plebe year at West Point, where it was an integral part of the general haze. Plebes had twenty physical education classes in four required activities: wrestling, boxing, swimming and gymnastics. I was a novice at all of these and trying to keep a passing grade was a yearlong struggle. There were three PE classes per week, and every other week there was a PE class on Saturday morning, along with math. Plus, there was a mile run indoors, a mile run in combat boots and fatigues, and a rope climb. I was below average in wrestling because I had little upper body strength at first—I was nearly 6 feet tall but weighed less than 150 pounds. I was put in the same weight class as plebes who were shorter and had lower centers of gravity, a disadvantage for a wrestler. But I did well enough to pass. Boxing was more terrifying than wrestling. We used large sixteen-ounce gloves and helmets. We were taught that for right handers, you kept your left arm extended for jabbing and for blocking jabs; when you saw an opening, you could try a right cross. Or an uppercut, which was the damaging type of blow. After a few training sessions, we had bouts, starting with a single one-minute round and working up to three rounds by the end. You have no idea how exhausting boxing is if you have never done it. On your toes, constantly moving, your arms with sixteen-ounce gloves held up, and trying to avoid getting knocked down. In one of my bouts, I caught my opponent on the chin with a right uppercut and he went down on his back. I was probably more surprised than he was. I have to admit, it was an exhilarating moment. I managed a B in boxing, which saved me in PE.

I sucked at swimming, though there were some interesting aspects. One test you had to pass was the "bob and travel." You jumped in the pool with fatigues, combat boots and a rifle. Then the idea was you would sink to the bottom of the ten foot pool, push off forward to the surface, and continue until you get to the other end of the pool. We were told that was how we might have to travel across rice paddies in Vietnam. I passed swimming, but with the equivalent of a D-. I out and out failed gymnastics. I had trouble with the most basic rolls, and when it came to the parallel bars and the pommel horse, I could not get started. What was more embarrassing was that the gymnastics instructor was also the freshman baseball coach, who I would later have to deal with as the team manager. But I was at least mediocre in boxing, and I could run well, so I passed PE.

One way Plebes could gain some respect in within their companies was through intramural sports. Everyone had to participate in intramurals. The first semester, I was assigned to the track team. I was not a sprinter. I was not much of a jumper either. But I found a niche running the half mile. I did well at some of the meets, coming in first or second at times and winning points for F! and the respect of the first classman who was the other F1 half-miler, Mr. Fogle.

Two months after school started, plebes in F1 had to move to another room in the same barracks. I had two new roommates, one from Louisiana and the other from Korea. I only remember the Korean roommate, Il-Soon Shin. He did not speak much English but was good at math, which did not require the same language skills as other classes. I can't imagine what it must have been like for him. We asked him what religion he was, thinking perhaps he was Buddhist, since we didn't really know much about Korean culture. He could not explain at the time, but the Academy designated him as Protestant, I assume by process of elimination—he was not Jewish and he wasn't Catholic. He became a standout in West Point's judo club.[11]

I previously mentioned the trials of trying to eat during Beast Barracks, and meals during the academic year were a long, dreary continuation. First, the same as in Beast Barracks, a plebe was assigned to stand by the stairs of the second floor and call out the uniform for the meal, which required him to consult the flagpole that identified the uniform. God help you if you came out in the wrong uniform, and even God could not come to the aid of a plebe who misjudged the uniform flag and called the wrong uniform for the entire company. All companies stood in formation outside for a role call and cadets marched to meals at the Washington Mess Hall in

---

11 Mr. Shin graduated from West Point in 1971 and by 2004 was a general in the South Korean army and the deputy commander of the South Korean Combined Forces. He was a professor at Inha University and is now a director of the Korea Electric Power Company. I always believed he had a bright future in his native country.

company formation. The Washington Mess Hall is enormous. One writer described it as a cross between a "Game of Thrones" and a "Harry Potter" set; personally, I would go more with the "Game of Thrones." It is gothic, medieval looking, stone, with six wings going out from a central area and a deck (unappetizingly known as the poop deck, "poop" being a term for new information).

For plebes, meals bordered on the obsessive, not because of the food but because of the hazing. Since there were close to 4,000 cadets while I was at West Point, that meant about 400 tables, each seating 10. There were company tables, for ordinary cadets, and then there were Corps Squad tables, for varsity athletes, including those on the plebe teams. At Corps Squad tables, the lucky plebe athletes were treated like humans. They did not have to brace; they could eat and they did not get hazed during meals. But only during their season; once that was over, the plebe was back on the company tables, out of practice with being victimized and at times at the mercy of upperclassmen who thought plebes on Corps Squad tables had it too easy.

All tables seated ten, with four on each side with one person at the head—a first classman, or firstie—and a hapless plebe at the other end. The tables included a mixture of all four classes. The plebe at the end rotated from day to day and was the "beverage corporal." Plebes were required to know the beverage preferences of the upperclassmen assigned to the table, which changed monthly. When table assignments were posted, the plebes at the table would summon the courage to knock on the door of an upperclassman's room and ask, in a loud voice, "Mr. X, sir, which are your beverage preferences?" Then, you'd try to make notes while standing at attention in the doorway, keeping the brace. In the background, the upperclassmen were snickering because they had suffered through the same hazing. I swear there were upperclassmen who went out of their way to make this difficult. "At breakfast, I want orange juice, a carton of milk and a glass of ice. At lunch I want ..." So you are scribbling these down while standing at attention, torn between wanting to make sure you got their preferences right and getting away from the upperclassman's room as soon as you could, because nothing good could come of being in an upperclassman's room. And God bless those few upperclassmen who said, "I'll let you know at the table."

At the table, the beverage corporal was expected to provide the beverages for the upperclassmen before he did anything else, starting with the head of the table and working down to the yearlings. At times, the beverage corporal sent the wrong beverage to the wrong person. That could bring a quick end to the hungry plebe's meal: "Donham, why don't you sit down there for a while and think about what my beverage preference for lunch is. Don't eat until I tell you."

Then, on to the meal, where you were looking straight ahead, still bracing and making sure you took one bite at a time, placing your fork down between bites. At any time, you could be interrupted with any number of questions and orders, such as being asked to recite one of a dozen items you were required to memorize from *Bugle Notes*. One I still remember is "How is the cow?" "Sir, she walks, she talks, she's full of chalk, the lacteal fluid extracted from the female of the bovine species is highly prolific to the nth degree"—"n" being the number of milk cartons on the table. (Math was extremely important at West Point.) Or you could be asked what the movies were for the coming weekend, or what the menu was for lunch or dinner, or, if your company had a parade that day, what marches were going to be played during the parade. If you failed to answer correctly, you would likely be told to sit at the table and think about it rather than eating. One of the worst things to keep track of was "the days"—a tradition in which plebes had to know the events of the week and the number of days until certain events, like graduation, which of course changed every day. You could never be sure what was coming your way during meals.

The food itself was pretty good, served family style. Wednesday night was almost always steak and potatoes. Lunch was sometimes an issue if you had some macaroni or spaghetti-like casserole, which sat in your stomach like a chunk of hot lead, especially if you had a boring class in a stuffy classroom right after the meal. For example, geography. It was so easy to fall asleep in class after one of those lunches. If you did, you were supposed to stand up in class. Once, there was a classmate in geography across the room from me trying to stay awake, standing and swaying next to an open window. I swear he almost fell out.

There was always a dessert, which at dinner occasionally included pie. Pie was another mealtime landmine, because one plebe at the table, known as the gunner, was responsible for cutting the pie into as many equal pieces as there were cadets at the table. Have you ever tried doing this? The supposed solution was to create a cardboard circular template using the protractor and slide rule that was standard equipment in every cadet room and draw lines extending from the center outward to the edge where there were marks 36 degrees apart, for example, in the case of 10 slices (360 degrees in a circle divided by 10). If you were the gunner, the idea was that you wrapped the template in a tissue and put it in your hat, and when it came time to cut the pie, you whisked the template out, set it down on the pie, and used it to cut your ten slices with mathematical precision. *Voila!* Practice often got in the way of theory, though.

You were nervous and self-conscious. You could miss the center. You could mismark the crust. Your template could be off a bit. You could be a lousy cutter. And any of these could mean involuntarily donating your piece of pie to the firstie at the head of the table.

Given these daily challenges, plebes over the years developed strategies to get permission to "fall out" at dinner—to relax the brace and stand or sit normally for a short time—and eat in relative peace. The most common was to perform a skit there in the mess hall, in the narrow spaces between tables. All it took was an idea, time for the plebes on the table to get together and plan the skit, get props into the mess hall under your uniform, remember what you were going to do and have a sympathetic and forgiving group of upperclassmen at the table. This occasionally worked. One Sunday afternoon, a plebe tablemate and I, who each played the guitar, sneaked our instruments into the mess hall. At the table, we announced that we were going to play a song, and my colleague, Chip Hindes, said that we were going to play a song I had written. The novelty worked. In fact, an upperclassman at the table, Jim Fouche, invited us to his room after dinner to discuss music and play us *Music from Big Pink*, the Band's first album.

One other generally successful, if not often used, gambit was to learn and recite the "Arkansas Poop," which was funny, vulgar and sophomoric—in other words, right up the alley of the upperclassmen at the table. (Remember, we were seventeen to twenty-one years old and more or less members of a campus-wide fraternity.) The premise of the "Arkansas Poop" is that the Arkansas legislature is considering a bill to change the name of Arkan*Saw* to Ar*Kansas*. Here is what I can remember:

Mr. Speaker, Mr. Speaker, you wall eyed son of a bitch. I'm the Honorable Senator Hiram P. Jones from Jackson County Arkansas, and I been standin' here for nigh onto half an hour while you been sitting up there like a hound dog with a cockle burr up your ass. Out of order, you say? Damn right I'm out of order. That's why I can only piss halfway across the Arkansas River. If I was in order, I could piss all the way across it. . . . change the name of Arkansaw? Why, that's like comparing the dangling dick of a Danish Duke to the minute meat of a Mongolian Monk! That's like comparing the ponderous pud of a Prussian Prince to the puny prick of a Polish priest! Change the name of Arkansaw?

Hell no; damn no!

What's not to like if you are a male between the ages of seventeen and twenty-one?

One of my ideas to get to eat was to try out as manager for the basketball team. Plebes who were on Corps Squad teams, the intercollegiate athletic teams, got to eat without hazing. Even managers. I didn't make it, but that effort did plant the seeds for a later more successful plan.

I never understood why West Point tolerated hazing at meals. Plebes were young men who had a physically and mentally demanding schedule along with constant pressure. We needed to eat if we were to perform to the potential we all had demonstrated to be admitted. Once again, tradition overcame common sense—until 1990, when hazing at West Point was officially eliminated.

CHAPTER 6:

FOOTBALL SEASON ENDS WITH NO SUGAR BOWL

The whole academy looked forward to the start of football season. Before the first game, there was a pep rally in Central Area, after taps, which to plebes was a big deal (before this, the only after-taps activity unofficially tolerated was studying secretly). I wrote my parents,

"Everyone runs out to Central Area in all kinds of crazy uniforms, and there are cheers, songs/the band plays/, and the captains talk. Everyone throws toilet paper and goes wild."

We especially looked forward to a trip to Boston College for an away game. When it actually happened, however, I found the trip discouraging. I used the several-hour bus ride home on October 1, 1967, to write my parents, expressing the feelings of most all the plebes I knew: "Well, the Boston trip is over, almost, and I'll soon be back at West Point. I don't really want to go back, but there isn't any choice. Getting away from the post lets you see a little of what you could be doing. What I mean is, when you get away and talk to kids from other schools and you're free, it's hard to want to go back to being a plebe. However, it isn't as bad as the beginning, by far.

At least I know where I'm going, and I'm used to it. It's hard not to regret being a civilian, though, when you get a taste of freedom."

Still, I was encouraged by academics after the first month and thought I might make the dean's list. One of the classes was Engineering Fundamentals, in which the first quarter was computer programming. These were the days of punch cards and the Fortran programming language, in which you punched out each step of the program on cards, fed them into the computer and hoped it would run. Of course, the computer was a mainframe, and you had to go to the library to punch the cards and run the program. I was very happy when I got my program, a simple do loop,[12] to run after only a couple tries. That was the high point of the class—when we got to the drafting part a few weeks later, I could not draw a straight line with a straightedge.

I marveled at cadets whose drawings and lettering looked almost God-like, they were so perfect. Mine more closely resembled snakes and my grade in that class tumbled end over end.

This is where I have to talk again about demerits. Demerits did not just afflict new plebes in Beast Barracks but were a general enforcement mechanism for all cadets. You could get demerits for your shoes being not shined well enough, for your belt buckle being smudged, for being late for formation, for not knowing something an upperclassman asked you, for your drawers in your room not being straight—pretty much for anything except having low grades in academics. More severe infractions (drinking or returning late from leave, for example) could lead to really large demerit awards. You were allowed a certain number a week. I have described walking the area during Beast Barracks, but it was worse during the fall, especially on a sunny Saturday afternoon. You could walk two hours on Friday

---

12 A "do loop" in Fortran, the computer language we were learning, is a command that runs a number of times.

and three on Saturday afternoon. While you were walking back and forth, back and forth, for three hours carrying your rifle on the shoulder, getting inspected (which carried the risk of picking up more demerits), the football game was going on up the hill and you could hear the crowd. It was aggravating because it was a wasted three hours. That was how I spent three weekends my first semester, before I learned how to avoid getting too many demerits. At least one of the football games was away, and the upperclassmen who were assigned to supervise the area—talk about a thankless task—played the football game on the radio over loudspeakers so us, beleaguered walkers, could listen. A belated thanks, whoever you were.

As the semester went on, I was focused on three things: my grades, Christmas vacation and getting off company tables. My grades were good, and I made the dean's list. Christmas vacation was getting closer.

My key to survival was to settle into a routine: studies, classes, intramurals, hazing, it all fit into a pattern. Time was moving by more quickly and involved constantly looking forward and looking back while surviving the present. The present was to be endured for the sake of the future. This was why plebes learning the "days" was so important to upperclassmen—everyone looked forward to getting out. "There are x days until the Army-Navy game; x days until Christmas vacation; x days until 500th night [until cows would graduate]; x days until 100th night and x days until graduation, sir." This was simply a fact of life at West Point. Only a few cadets loved academy life, and for the life of me I couldn't understand why. You defended West Point to the outside world. You believed you were making a difference for the country through the training. You knew you were being tested more than the vast majority of college students were being tested. You gradually got used to academy life. But you didn't love it. Kind of like Groucho Marx in *Go West* at Grand Central Station with Harpo, running into Chico:

Chico: Who's he?

Groucho: He's my brother.

Chico: So you love him, right?

Groucho: No, but I'm used to him.

Cadets gradually got used to cadet life.

You might wonder what weekends were like, other than Saturday morning classes, possibly walking the area, parades and football games, which were over by about 3pm on Saturday afternoon. For me, during plebe year, they were often lonely. Here I was, 17, struggling to make sense of military/college life, 1,000 miles from home and trying to get by. "Sometimes I think weekends are worse than the week," I wrote to my parents. "This may be hard to explain, but I think I can. All through the week you look forward to one thing: the weekend. Then it's here, and all of a sudden, what do you have to look forward to? The next week, with its studies, intramurals, etc. Sometimes, weekends are really bad."

That same weekend, I went to see *The Sound of Music* at Thayer Hall, where there were movies on Saturday night. It was a new release, and it helped take my mind off the daily grind. Plus, the story of the von Trapp family taking a stand against the Nazis and crossing the Alps to safety felt like a metaphor for plebe year. These days, I am addicted to murder mysteries, but I still can watch *The Sound of Music*.

Some weekends, there also were dances (or hops, as they were known before hops became associated with IPAs) where girls from nearby women's colleges, like Vassar in Poughkeepsie or Ladycliff in Highland Falls, were bussed in. Sometimes, the band was from the US Army band at West Point, one of the best bands in the Army. Sometimes, they were cadet bands. By the end of the year, a band of Plebes I was in played at a couple of the hops.

On the other hand (there was always another hand in cadet life), every month or so, plebes in your company were tapped for guard duty. You were assigned to a guard a barracks on Saturday night, walking the halls in a dress gray uniform for two or three hours making sure cadets weren't drinking or having girls in their rooms. This was an exquisite way to waste a good Saturday night. Occasionally, an upperclassman confined to his room or behind in studies would play music with the door slightly open. At this point in first-semester plebe life, we were not allowed to have stereos in our rooms. I still associate "Build Me Up Buttercup" with Saturday night guard duty. This was just one of those things plebes like me had to adjust to. As usual, I complained to my parents: "So many things have happened, and it's been hard to adjust to a completely new way of life. Really, I still haven't yet. It's still hard for me to do everything the way I'm supposed to because so much of it seems ridiculous; there seems to be so little reason for most of it. There are many times I'd like to forget about shining shoes, but of course, I can't. But I guess in the long run it's worth it." That was a cadet's hope and wish—that in the long run, it would be worth it.

By mid-October, I was closely following Army sports, I was doing well in classes, and I was seventy-four days from Christmas vacation. I told my parents: "There are some things about West Point that have surprised me. One is that many cadets don't seem to care about the grades they get as long as they pass. . . . Another is the number of people at the parades. Yesterday, there were people standing around the plain—the bleachers were packed—just to watch a parade. I don't see why but I guess the full-dress parades must be something to see."

You cannot underestimate the importance to cadets, and especially plebes, of the Army-Navy football game It meant a weekend trip in late November for the entire Corps to Philadelphia, where the game is traditionally held. Plebes were especially excited because not only was this a trip away from West Point for just the second time since July, but also if Army beat Navy, all plebes could fall out in the mess hall until Christmas. And this looked like a good bet as October moved into November.

Army's football team was steadily improving as the season went on. After it shut out Utah 22-0 on Veteran's Day, November 11, 1967 (also my eighteenth birthday), it was 7-1, with wins over Stanford, SMU and Air Force Academy, and with two games to go. The first of those was Pitt, which was having a poor season, and then the season would close with Navy. There were widespread reports that Army would be invited to the Sugar Bowl in New Orleans. Both Navy and Air Force had participated before in bowl games, but not Army. Now, West Point had a chance to be the third service academy to go to a bowl game. Cadets, including me, were calculating how to cut their Christmas leaves at home short and go to the game.

However, just days before Army's game against Pitt, Stanley Resor, Secretary of the Army (who I later sued) ruled against Army participating in any bowl games, including the Sugar Bowl. The disappointment was palpable. One morning, it was discovered that cadets had removed over 300 sugar bowls from the mess hall overnight in protest. The decision also appeared to demoralize the football team, which barely squeaked out a win against Pitt. Then, to add injury to insult, Army lost to Navy, which had lost its previous three games. This was a disheartening time for the Corps, especially for plebes. Not only was there no falling out in the mess hall, but upperclassmen took out their own disappointment on us. I was relieved when Christmas leave finally arrived.

"There's something happening here, what it is ain't exactly clear
Buffalo Springfield, "For What It's Worth" 1967

During my first year at West Point, I helped form a plebe rock band. It actually started during Beast Barracks when a few of us met, threw a few songs together and played at the end of summer plebe hike—I was surprised that there were other plebes who had played in bands in high school. We did not have much time to rehearse, so we played popular songs that were simple and that everybody kind of knew: "Louie Louie" (about which Bruce Springsteen says nobody really knows the supposedly obscene lyrics), "Good Lovin'," "Little Bit of Soul," "Double Shot of My Baby's Love"— the kind of songs Springsteen later called fraternity rock. We finally played at a few freshman dances. In its own way, as I mentioned, West Point back then was kind of like an exclusive fraternity, except with no drinking, no girls (except on weekends), no parties.

There were occasional concerts, though. In particular, the Beach Boys, Buffalo Springfield, and the Soul Survivors (remember "Expressway to Your Heart"?) played at West Point over Thanksgiving weekend. They played in the field house, a large, acoustically demented building away from the main campus. You could barely hear, but it was the real Buffalo Springfield, Stephen Stills, Neil Young and the rest. It was an interesting juxtaposition, the band in fringed leather jackets and long hair with an audience of uniformed cadets. I have always wondered what they were thinking. The Beach Boys were the headliners, of course. They came out wearing Hawaiian shirts. It was interesting to see one of them make the weird sound in "Good Vibrations" with a theremin, although I had no idea back then what a theremin was.

Another concert the first year was a then-popular band, Jay and the Americans.

Playing in the band was one of my main entertainments during plebe year and in later years. Maybe that should have been another sign I was in the wrong place, but I wasn't alone. There were probably three or four cadet rock bands that practiced when they could and played at dances when there was a chance.

CHAPTER 7

ONE SEMESTER DOWN, ONE TO GO

I went home for Christmas, flying from Newark to Lambert Airport in St. Louis, where my parents met me. It was good to be home, but it was a very short visit. I visited some friends who had continued the band I had been in, which was now known as the Umbrella Factory. They played me a new artist, Jimi Hendrix, and his song "Purple Haze." I had no idea what purple haze was, but the song was catchy. (Still is.) Then back to West Point, where nothing had changed. (Never had and probably never would.) No one was glad to be back, and the first thing everyone started wondering was "How long till spring leave?"

By the end of the first semester, I was on the dean's list, and I caught a break academically—or so I thought. In my American literature class, I had picked James Fenimore Cooper as an author and was supposed to read four of his novels. (I didn't; I skimmed them and read the Cliff Notes.) We had to write two papers. My first, which my professor approved, compared Natty Bumppo, the "noble savage" in Cooper's *Leatherstocking Tales*, to hippies. My professor liked it and gave me an A. The second, which my professor also approved, discussed how Natty Bumppo would have reacted to the Vietnam War. I again received an A. I was one of the top plebe students in English, and I got validated out of second-semester freshman

English into sophomore world literature. This meant that I would have an additional elective in future years.

Be careful what you wish for. Unlike my first-semester English professor, a Lieutenant Colonel who was more or less a permanent English professor at West Point, my world literature professor, Captain Beasley, had recently returned from Vietnam and was young and gung-ho. Our first reading was the *Iliad*. Being cocky after my creative essays the first semester, my proposed first essay on the *Iliad* was to compare the Trojan War to the war in Vietnam. It seemed like there were many similarities, and I had the paper sketched out in my mind.[13] In the *Iliad*, the Greeks have been bogged down for years besieging Troy with no clear end in sight. By 1967, the US had been in Vietnam for at least six years, and there was no clear win to the war in sight. During the Trojan War as Homer described it, there was no clear strategy, and the battles between the Trojans and the Greeks went back and forth with no side gaining a clear advantage. The same seemed true in Vietnam. In fact, as we have since learned, it was truer than we cadets even suspected at the time, since the National Liberation Front actually controlled a large amount of rural Vietnam and had become much better armed, mostly through obtaining American weapons from ARVN, the South Vietnamese government troops. I assumed that since I had been successful in using current events in connection with my James Fenimore Cooper essays, my proposal would be accepted and even complimented. I was shocked when gung-ho Captain Beasley flatly rejected my proposed topic. I could not understand why, since I had given it a lot of thought. I don't believe he gave a reason, and of course there was no way a plebe could question a professor's judgment. We were the very bottom link on the chain of command.

---

13 In 1994, Dr. Jonathon Shay published a book, "Achilles in Vietnam: Combat Trauma and the Undoing of Character," which made a similar comparison based on Dr. Shay's treatment of returning Vietnam veterans.

I was left to come up with something else at the last minute and submitted a paper that seemed adequate but not exceptional. I was shocked again when I got a C, meaning that I had gone from among the top of my class in English to the middle, and I could not understand what I had done to piss off Captain Beasley. About ten years later, it finally hit me that my proposed paper hit too close to home. He must have thought I was questioning his service—and it was not my place, as a plebe, to question his service, and it was not my place to question the Vietnam War. Maybe this, too, should have been an early warning as to my career path. But it wasn't. I just dug in and raised my grade to a B+ by the end of the semester.

In early 1968, the war talk around West Point, for a few days was not about the Vietnam War. Rather, it was about North Korea's capture of the USS *Pueblo*. I had forgotten about this sorry episode until I read a letter to my parents dated January 25, 1968, which described North Korea as "the big topic around here." What is more interesting is that my letters home do not mention the Tet Offensive in South Vietnam, which started around January 31, 1968, and has been described as a turning point in the Vietnam War. I don't remember the Tet Offensive being discussed.

The rest of the second semester seemed to go by more quickly than the first semester. I was able to buy a stereo and records. (I remember Crosby, Stills and Nash; Neil Young; the Beatles; and Three Dog Night.) Getting access to music was a big deal for plebes, partly because it offered some freedom—the freedom to play the music you wanted during the times it was allowed and when roommates agreed. It also was a signal that plebe year was slowly passing. At the same time, there seemed to be a slight slackening of upperclassmen's desire to harass plebes. After all, firsties were looking forward to graduation, and cows were approaching 500 days from graduation. And I was named one of the student managers of the plebe baseball team, which meant I got to sit at "Corps Squad" tables and not have to brace while eating. From that point on, plebe life was better. My grades were good, and my roommate's girlfriend introduced me to a young woman with long red hair who came to visit a few weekends and occasionally sent me cookies. By May 1968, I wrote home that "the Plebe system is kind of deteriorating and it's just about all over."

By the end of plebe year, I had As in all my 40.5 first-year credit hours except for Engineering Fundamentals, Geography of Latin America (maybe the most boring course I took at West Point), English, Fundamentals of Military Operations and PE. I thought I had done pretty well.

—

The first week of June was a red-letter day: graduation in Michie Stadium. The firsties were in full dress uniform on the football field while the rest of the Corps and the guests were in the stands. General Harold K. Johnson, then Army Chief of Staff, made a speech; then, one by one the graduates stepped to the podium in class rank order to receive their diplomas. There was a huge cheer for the goat, the grad with the lowest class rank (in notable contrast to how GOAT now means "greatest of all time"). Class rank does not necessarily speak to one's future success—John McCain was the goat of his Naval Academy class. Then the class of 1968 was dismissed. All the grads threw their hats in the air and we plebes were plebes no more. We were "recognized," in West Point lingo, by the upperclassmen, who shook the hands of those they had harassed during the previous nine months. We did not have to brace anymore. We did not have to recite at the whim of random upperclassmen anymore. We did not have to worry about meals. We had become members of the club.

Right after June Week, plebes had a four-week leave. I went home, wore civilian clothes, and saw a few high school friends but was a bit bored. I managed to hitch a flight from Scott Air Force Base on a C-141 to

McChord Air Force base near Tacoma, Washington, to visit my roommate Les LeMieux. It was an awful flight, sitting on a seat that pulled down from the wall of the cavernous, noisy plane, but it was free. It was my first trip out west. We saw the Space Needle, took a day trip to Vancouver, Canada, and caught a distant view of Mt. Rainier. After a week, I flew back to Scott the same way, hitching a ride on a C-141 from McChord, and all too soon it was back to West Point for my summer at Camp Buckner.

CHAPTER 8:

CAMP BUCKNER: THE BEST SUMMER OF A CADET'S CAREER?

What did you learn in school today, dear little boy of mine?

I learned that war is not so bad, I learned about the great ones we have had

We fought in Germany and in France and someday I might get my chance

That's what I learned in school today, that's what I learned in school.

Tom Paxton, "What Did You Learn in School Today"

Camp Buckner is a training camp on the United States Military Academy reservation on Lake Popolopen.[14] It is named for General Simon Bolivar Buckner, Jr., a former commandant of cadets who was killed in action in January 1945 during the battle for Okinawa in World War II. At first glance, Camp Buckner is a peaceful setting, but the peaceful view

---

14 In 2020, first-class men and women ordered to return to West Point during the COVID-19 pandemic to be the audience for a graduation speech by President Trump were first to quarantine for fourteen days at Camp Buckner. I can't express just how much requiring soon-to-be-commissioned officers to return to West Point in the midst of a pandemic disgusted me.

could be deceiving given the military training that occurs there. The barracks and mess hall are within walking distance of the lake. While the barracks, large single rooms with bunk beds for about twenty yearlings and a latrine, were more rustic than those at the academy "campus," the fact that we did not have to brace or worry about saluting upperclassmen made the physical setting no big deal. Plus, having survived plebe year, we were a bit cocky.

We were told that Camp Buckner would be the best summer of our cadet careers. That was a very low bar. We were to have a week's training in the combat arms: infantry, armor, artillery, signal corps, engineering. Then there was the RECONDO week, an introduction to Ranger training.

Once we arrived, what did our Camp Buckner training entail? For infantry, "the training was pretty good—squad and platoon in the attack, and platoon defense; also night patrols. We had classes, practice attacks using blank ammunition," I wrote to my parents. We also were given the opportunity (?) to fire fully automatic M-16s (our usual rifles were M-14s, which were semi-automatic) and M 60 machine guns. There also was an obstacle course called the "confidence course." It involved some sort of climb, and the cadet in front of me fell, which shook my confidence. But whatever it was, I successfully climbed twenty-five feet. We had instructor training, where we learned the Army three step method of instruction: tell them what you are going to tell them, tell them, and then tell them what you told them. We had day and night compass courses, where we were given coordinates for six points and sent out into the woods, where we had to find trees with letters on them, copy the letters and return for the reward of not being made to feel like an idiot. We found all the coordinates but walked ten miles that day.

Artillery training was at a range near the camp. Because the 105 mm howitzer, the Army's main artillery weapon in the Vietnam War, had an effective range of about 7 miles, the range had both a firing area and a target area. The target area looked like a lunar landscape from the years of cadets learning how to kill people miles away. We were taught about being a forward observer and calling in coordinates for targets, how to aim and adjust 105 mm howitzers and how to fire them at targets. Targeting artillery was trial and error, known as "bracketing." The forward observer would radio back if the first shell was short or over the target. The soldiers firing the howitzer would adjust the range based on that information and keep trying until they hit the target while the forward observer did his best to stay safe and out of sight. We also fired mortars, which involved getting the mortar adjusted, dropping in the shell and making damn sure your head was out of the way. I distinctly recall a lieutenant who was training us dropping a shell in the mortar, which did not fire immediately. After a couple of seconds, he started to lean down to look in the mortar when it fired, just missing blowing his head off. Lesson learned! I don't recall being taught about collateral damage, which is what happened when you missed a target, but it should have been, as it was a major issue in the Vietnam War.

For the armor training, we went to Ft. Knox, which not only has a cache of gold but also, at least in 1968, was one of the Army's primary armor bases. I learned how to drive and fire a tank and to drive an armored personnel carrier (APC). Steering a tank is not that hard. The one I drove had a T-bar, and it reminded me of steering a tricycle, if the tricycle weighed about 50 tons and carried a 105 mm gun and a secondary machine gun. It had a crew of four—a driver, a gunner, and a loader/radio operator—plus the tank commander, who sometimes rode standing with his upper body outside the tank. The inside was claustrophobic, hot and noisy and smoky when the main gun was fired. I felt pretty safe about being inside a tank until we were shown the LAW, the disposable light antitank weapon that you could carry on your back and fire from your shoulder.[16]

We understood that tanks were not the weapon of choice in Vietnam. They were for repelling a communist invasion of Western Europe, this being the time of the Cold War.

APCs, however, were used in Vietnam, and we rode in and drove them too. They could transport infantry soldiers to the front more quickly and safely than walking and, at least theoretically, could move through rice paddies and forest terrain that would deter most other vehicles. The most dangerous role in the APC was of the soldier responsible for the machine gun, who had to ride on the top. At the time, there was something intoxicating about the power of the artillery and armor military machines, a sense of invulnerability. We were not told about how the National Liberation Front had stymied APCs in rice paddies at the 1963 battle of Ap Bac, which Neil Sheehan later wrote about in *A Bright Shining Lie* and Ken Burns vividly described in his PBS series on the Vietnam War. I suppose it is possible that our instructors didn't even know details about Ap Bac, since the official story was that it was a great victory for the US.

I don't remember a lot about Signal Corps and engineering. Signal Corps back then handled communications, which were pretty rudimentary compared to now. For engineering, we had to create a pontoon bridge, but I don't remember out of what.

The culmination of Camp Buckner training was RECONDO. Here is how I described it:

> Well RECONDO is over. It was a fast week. It's hard to
> describe it, in the same way that Beast was hard to describe.
> It started Monday at 0100, when everyone got up. By 0200
> we had started our march (over hills and through woods)
> to the base camp. We got there at about 0530, ate break-
> fast and set up tents. At 0800, we had 2 hours in the pits,

sawdust pits, for hard-to-hand combat. It was a real haze. Then, a 1.7 mile run (and walk) uphill to the mountaineering site. There we learned to repel off cliffs. Everyone made a 25-foot and a 65-foot repel. It was pretty much fun. That night we had a survival class and then a road march back to the camp. Next day, we had a patrolling class first, then 2 more hrs. in the pits (in a pouring rain). After dinner we made a 1.3 mile run to the stream crossing site and we learned to make a poncho raft + 1 rope bridge. That night there was a walk through patrol. The next morning at 0400, everyone got up and we left for a 2 day patrol. It was like being a platoon in a combat situation for 2 days. Friday, was the slide-for-life and log walk; then it was over.

There was a little more to RECONDO that was not in my letter. At one evening camp, we watched a Ranger bite the head off a chicken. (I thought that was impressive until I saw Baker Mayfield bite a beer can and chug it.) A lieutenant who was part of the rappelling training fell and was killed, and on Friday morning, a number of cadets went to his memorial service.

Of course, I don't know to what extent the two-day platoon patrol was really like being in a combat situation. Certainly, we did not face the terror of an ambush or a booby trap or being fired at, and we knew it would be over in two days. We knew there was no real objective we had to take. We assumed we would not be coming back in a body bag—although the death at the rappelling site was a reminder that RECONDO was not without risk. We expected the worst that would happen might be a sprained ankle or a bruised knee from running into one of the low rock walls that seemed to thread everywhere across the woods near Camp Buckner. But from talking to a friend who was a second lieutenant and platoon leader in Vietnam, what was similar was the confusion, the obstacles you could not see, and your dependence on your squad, none of whom likely knew any more than you did but who might have known more than a recently commissioned second lieutenant platoon leader. We were all trying to do the patrol right, to be good soldiers.

The slide for life was a fitting end to the week. Cadets line up to climb a vertical wooden ladder about fifty to sixty feet high. There is a backup on the ladder as the cadet at the top prepares for the slide, so you spend fifteen minutes or so climbing and hanging on the ladder. At the top, you grab with both hands a bar that is attached to a cable extending from the top of the tower to the shore of the other side of Lake Popolopen. With a signal from the other side, you step off and hold on the pulley and slide all the way across the lake, and with another signal you let go and drop into the lake near the far shore. Then you get out of the water, climb another ladder about twenty feet up, and walk across a two-by-four until you reach a two or three foot barrier. You step across the barrier onto a log, walk about another ten feet or so and on another signal, drop twenty feet into the lake again and swim a short distance back to the shore in your fatigues and combat boots. Then, RECONDO was done. We were ready to fight. And the "best summer" of this cadet's career ended.

WE MISSED THE LONG HOT SUMMER OF 1968

Outside West Point, 1968 was one of the most troubled years in recent memory. The Vietnam War was dragging on. Even Secretary McNamara had secretly advised President Johnson the previous year that the war was turning into a quagmire: "I see no reasonable way to bring the war to an end soon. Enemy morale has not broken—he apparently has adjusted to our stopping his drive for military victory and has adopted a strategy of keeping us busy and waiting us out (a strategy of attriting our national will)."[15]

McNamara further wrote to the president that the political strategy of "pacification" had been a "bad disappointment," that the Rolling Thunder campaign of bombing North Vietnam had not been successful and that, if anything, the status of the war was 'worse off' than before."

1968 turned out to be the bloodiest year of the war for the US military. Nearly 17,000 soldiers were killed. On January 31, the United States was surprised by the Tet Offensive, a massive attack by the National Liberation Front (Viet Cong) on most Vietnamese cities. The attack came perilously close to taking Saigon, and the NLF did take control of Hue for several months. CBS news anchor Walter Cronkite flew to Vietnam in February and, on February 27, reported in a now famous telecast that the outcome of the Tet Offensive may be judged by historians not as a victory for the US or the NLF but as a military draw. The Tet Offensive decimated the NLF but led to North Vietnam becoming more involved in the war and changed the American approach to the war.[16] On March 31, the US stopped its relentless bombing campaign of North Vietnam in hopes of starting peace negotiations. That same day, President Johnson announced he would not run for re-election.

On April 24, Martin Luther King was assassinated in Memphis. Riots in over 100 cities followed, leaving 39 people dead. Robert Kennedy entered the Democratic race for the presidential nomination but was assassinated on TV on June 5, after winning the California primary. The United States began a long series of fruitless peace talks with North Vietnam, with a lame duck president and an electorate sharply divided over the war. The Democratic convention, held in Chicago in late August, turned into riots

---

15 Pentagon Papers
16 Sheehan, *Bright Shining Lie*

79

when police and National Guard troops rushed protesters and reporters, with Mayor Daley memorably saying, "The police are not here to create disorder; they are here to preserve disorder." The convention then nominated Senator Hubert Humphrey, who lost to Republican Richard Nixon. Nixon claimed he had plan to end the war, which he never described during the 1968 Presidential campaign, but it turned out largely to be what became known as "Vietnamization." This involved placing far more fighting responsibility on the South Vietnamese Army. Anti-war activists referred to Vietnamization, accurately, as changing the color of the corpses. It also turned out Nixon sabotaged Paris peace talks during his 1968 campaign by secretly urging the South Vietnamese to walk away.

Back at West Point, however, these events took a back seat to academics and the routine struggle of cadet life.

CHAPTER 9:

YEARLING YEAR

Reorganization Week again was a hassle, even though I had been through it once. As usual, we had to locate uniforms and other stuff we had stored in the barracks basement for the summer, meet and get acquainted with new roommates and organize a new room. But it was surely much less of a hassle than the year before as a plebe.

Having survived Reorganization Week number two, we were back at the academy campus and immersed in academics. It was a serious relief not to be hazed. Most yearlings tried to help plebes through some of the rough transition from high school through Beast Barracks into academic year life where possible. On the other hand, we were expected to uphold the plebe system, especially in Company F-1, where I remained. There was some tension, but compared to the previous year, it was no sweat. Plus, we had our stereos at the beginning of the year, we had one weekend leave a semester, and there was a sense of freedom—to the extent that being a bird in a much larger cage is freedom.

However, yearling, or sophomore, year was a bear academically. I had 22.5 credit hours a semester, including advanced calculus, advanced physics ("physics is physics with calculus; advanced physics is calculus with physics"), advanced chemistry, advanced French, a military course, history and economics. My course load was no different from that of any other yearlings except not all cadets were in advanced sections. Interestingly, the course that I recall the most now, and has given me the most useful information, is economics. Math was very difficult, and I have no idea how I got a B the first semester. I did well in physics, but physics has changed so much over the last fifty years that what was advanced in 1968 is high school stuff now. What I learned in economics, as it relates to supply and demand, the classic "guns vs. butter" illustrations in the Paul Samuelson textbook, still serves as a basis for understanding the world. That said, I still remember from my military tactics class the "Plan of Attack"; the first rule is know your enemy.

That fall semester, I ended up on the F-1 intramural orienteering team. Orienteering is a combination of cross country and map and compass reading. Two-man teams were given coordinates and a compass, and headed out into the back woods of the West Point base to find trees with numbers on them, which we had to write down and return with before other teams did. The sites were about two miles apart. I was teamed with a first classman named Bob Anderson, a very good man who had spent a year at Purdue before transferring to West Point.[17] We did well, winning the regimental championship, which means we were first among the eight First Regiment companies. Orienteering two times a week was a grind at the end of a long day of academics, and coming in first was something to be proud of. And I certainly didn't have to worry about not eating.

I followed football season, but Army wasn't as good as its great team from 1967. I, like all cadets, was pleased when Army beat Navy in Philadelphia. I had bet some unknown midshipman a bathrobe. If I won,

---

17 Bob Anderson joined the infantry after graduating in 1969. He became an airborne Ranger and served for eighteen months in Vietnam as well as an advisor to the State Department. He later served in the CIA and then in private industry until his death from cancer in 2005.

I would receive a Naval Academy bathrobe. If Army lost, an unknown midshipman would receive a West Point bathrobe courtesy of my bank account. I gave the bathrobe I won to my father. I got it back after he passed away, and I still have it. It is navy (of course) blue with gold trim, wool and really scratchy.

I was looking forward to physical education in the second semester of yearling year because I had signed up for skiing. West Point had a small hill that served the dual purpose of being a challenge to new cadets to climb up during training hikes and actually serving as a ski slope for cadets, officers and their guests in the winter. There are no ski slopes in southern Illinois, and learning to ski seemed like an opportunity to step outside my comfort zone. After two or three lessons I was learning the snowplow and one Friday, after class, I went to the ski slope to practice. There was a very mild "baby" slope that I was doing pretty well on. Next to it was a slope with about the same incline but with a few trees. I was cold, and there was a yearling event that night, but I told myself just one more run. I decided to tackle the tree slope. Bad move. I ran into a tree and hobbled off the slope in pain. But I went to the event that night because I had a date and danced the night away. The next day I could barely walk and went on sick call. I was diagnosed with a hematoma on my right knee, which just would not bend. I was on crutches for a couple of weeks, and it was more than a month before I could walk normally. I have not been on a ski slope since.

During the second semester, my roommate Les LeMieux, who was also the drummer in the cadet rock bands I was in, started dating a young woman from Ladycliff College, Paddy Quinlan, from nearby Nyack, New York. Ladycliff was in Highland Falls, the town adjacent to the south of West Point. It was a small Catholic girls' school that, while often derided by cadets as a "lesser than" school compared with nearby Vassar, was nonetheless the source of many dates, trysts and marriages for graduating cadets due to its proximity.

Les was very bright, and we had become good friends since plebe year. He was about 5'8" with a wiry build. Paddy was slim and short and was always upbeat, and she seemed to be the epitome of a serious and faithful Catholic young woman. Keep in mind that, having grown up Methodist in a small town where there was little interaction between Catholics and "publics," I had little experience even talking to Catholic women. During the spring, Les asked me if I would go on a blind date with one of Paddy's friends, Diane Parus. As I recall, Les and Paddy described Diane as a math major, very bright but somewhat troubled. I agreed.

This turned out to be a very significant date for Diane and me—both good and, then later, bad. Diane and I hit it off. She was troubled by what she described as a bad relationship in high school. She also talked about an aunt who had serious drinking problem and her disgust with seeing her aunt's house, which was overrun with cockroaches. Looking back, Diane probably was depressed, but depression was not a common topic in 1969. Who knows, I may have been depressed too, but probably many cadets are depressed a bit in the middle of winter at West Point, where it's cold and snowy, it gets dark early and the day-to-day grind starts to wear.

Diane turned out to be not only a math major but also an avid reader and introduced me to books such as *A Separate Peace* and *Siddhartha*. We would meet on weekends and occasionally talk on the phone during the week. She started writing frequent letters in a small blue hand on textured paper. Unlike today, when cadets have email accounts, there was either elation or discouragement after mail call, because many cadets were waiting for letters from girlfriends or from home. Mail call was a daily chance for momentary happiness if a letter arrived or, more often, disappointment if one didn't.

Diane was also a Catholic and said she had once considered becoming a nun. I think I assumed all Catholic girls said they briefly considered becoming nuns, but I had the sense Diane was serious. The fact that we both were serious about religion was something we had in common. We went on a weekend leave together and saw Peter, Paul and Mary at a concert in White Plains. All of a sudden I was involved in a serious relationship—serious enough that I even told my parents about Diane. By the end of our sophomore years, we were falling in love.

Meanwhile, I continued to do well in my classes and stayed on the dean's list. In advanced math, I met my match in multi-dimensional geometry. I could never get my head around a saddle-shaped universe. Still I survived, but it was a struggle. All I remember from that part of sophomore math is that an integral calculates the area under a line or a curve. That was bad enough, but integrals in three or four dimensions—help!

Finishing yearling year was significant. Not only had I succeeded in making it through Beast Barracks, I had also been trained in all the combat arms, had an introduction to Ranger training, and presumably was poised to continue becoming an instrument for accomplishing the current focus of American foreign policy: winning the intractable Vietnam War. Academically, after two years of college, I had earned eighty-five credit hours, which in most colleges would have almost been enough to complete three years.

However, once a cadet started the summer of junior year, he was committed. If he left West Point after junior year began without graduating, he owed the Army two years of service, starting at the enlisted rank of specialist 4th class. If he left after senior year started without graduating, he owed the Army three years, starting at the rank of specialist 4th class. Neither seemed a good option. This meant the end of sophomore year was a decision point. "Should I stay or should I go?" was on many of my classmates' minds, and mine, long before the Clash sang about that. There were many considerations. If I left, would it be because I just couldn't "take it"? I had done well for two years, so I knew I could survive. If I left, I would go back in the draft. June 1969 was before the first lottery in December 1969, so I would have to enroll in some other college to avoid 1A status. But that would mean retreating back to New Baden and enrolling at University of Illinois, a thousand miles away from Diane. No part of that was appealing. Plus, I was about to complete the two hardest years at West Point—Beast Barracks and plebe year and yearling academics would all be behind me. And leaving would have this sense of failure.

In one sense, I was operating under Newton's first law of motion—a body at rest or in motion continues to stay at rest or in motion unless acted on by an outside force. After successfully finishing yearling year, there was no outside force pushing me to leave. My academic class rank was improving. Diane was going to be in a college next door to West Point for two more years. Like most cadets, I felt like the hardest part of the West Point experience was over.

The next decision was how I would spend the summer either before or after a month of leave. Some rising juniors and seniors would spend a month touring various Army bases across the country. The juniors who did not go on the tour and the seniors who had gone on the tour the summer before would crucify new cadets during Beast Barracks. Even then, there were two options: the first was to greet the new cadets as they entered the Central Area and start their introduction into cadet life; the second was to work the second half of Beast Barracks, which involved longer hikes and more physical training. Either way, as a junior I would be either a squad leader or an assistant squad leader, responsible for either beginning or finishing the Beast Barracks training of eleven new cadets. I chose to go to Beast Barracks and was assigned to the second half.

Sadly, for me anyway, Les decided to leave. I think he was just done with the aggravation. He resigned at the end of the year. His wedding with Paddy was set for August.

After graduation for the class of 1969, I went home for a couple of weeks, and then visited Diane in Rochester, New York, where I met her family. Her father was a fine man who worked, I believe, for Kodak. (Diane described Rochester as a suburb of Kodak—how times change.) Her mom was a severe Polish woman who worked in a factory. I did learn from Diane's mother how to make golumbke, or stuffed cabbage. Diane had a younger brother, John, who eventually graduated from the Naval Academy and retired from the navy after twenty years as an officer. She also had a younger sister, Patti.

Yearling year seemed like a turning point. I was succeeding in academics and I had passed through RECONDO, one of the physically toughest West Point experiences. I had driven a tank, fired a howitzer, and handled and fired an M 60 machine gun although in rather antiseptic circumstances. Diane and I were growing closer, especially after Les resigned and Paddy quit Ladycliff. I knew I could make it to graduation. I decided to stay.

CHAPTER 10:

DIVING INTO THE RIVER—THE SPIRIT OF THE BAYONET RETURNS

"War has its evils. In all ages it has been the minister of wholesale death
and appalling desolation; but however inscrutable to us, it has also
been made, by the All-wise Dispenser of events, the instrumentality
of accomplishing the great end of human elevation and human
happiness."—Howard Zinn, "Peoples' History of the United States", p. 155,
quoting Senator H.V. Johnson on the Mexican War[18]

I returned to West Point around the end of July. I was a squad leader of
eleven new cadets. They were all bright and intelligent young men, and my
job was to train and nurture them through the end of Beast Barracks, getting them ready for the academic year—a balance of being as encouraging
as possible but making sure they understood that self-discipline was key to
survival. Aside from the manual of arms, two of the drills I was required to

---

18 Sen. Johnson served, from Georgia, was a slave owner who served in the Senate from
1848–1849. Thereafter, he became Governor of Georgia and a senator in the Confederacy.
He did not serve in the military in either the Mexican War or the Civil War, proving again
that talk is cheap.

lead were rifle exercises and bayonet drills. For each, squad leaders had an outline of what we were to say and what the result of the training should be. Enthusiasm, not necessarily skill, was the focus. A 1919 book, "Koehler's West Point Manual of Disciplinary Physical Training," explained that the "object of the Rifle Exercises [is] to develop the muscles of the arms, shoulders, and back so the men become accustomed to the weight of the piece and learn to wield it so the 'handiness' so essential to its use in firing, bayonet training and in the manual of arms becomes second nature. When these exercises are combined with movements of the various other parts of the body, they serve as a very efficient, though a rather strenuous, method of all around development." The M14 rifle, which all cadets were issued and responsible for back then, weighed about 8.5 pounds. Does that seem light? Well, try holding 8.5 pounds out in front of you at arm's length, then raising it over your head 20 times or so. Then, lift it over your head; move it to the right, bending the opposite arm; then back to the center, then to the left, etc. There were any number of variations. Then, to close, just hold the damn thing in front of you for a minute or so. These exercises could be grueling, especially for eighteen-year-old men who were already exhausted from stress and too little sleep. I had no issue leading rifle exercises, which were just physical fitness exercises, without any obvious moral component.

On the other hand, leading bayonet drill was the beginning of my path toward requesting discharge as a conscientious objector. As the squad leader, I stood on a platform in the middle of an open field with my squad in front of me, with other squad leaders from first company similarly situated on the training field. Bayonet drill was at Target Hill field, near the intramural track and field area in a low area not far from the Hudson River. This part of the West Point campus is not readily visible to the sightseeing public until fall, when it can be used for Army football game parking. As

West Point was partially open to the public, I suspect that holding bayonet drill away from public scrutiny was deliberate.

A United States War Department Field Manual on bayonet training states:

> **THE SPIRIT OF THE BAYONET** The will to meet and destroy the enemy in hand-to-hand combat is the spirit of the bayonet. It springs from the fighter's confidence, courage, and grim determination, and is the result of vigorous training. Through training, the fighting instinct of the individual soldier is developed to the highest point. The will to use the bayonet first appears in the trainee when he begins to handle it with facility, and increases as his confidence grows. The full development of his physical prowess and complete confidence in his weapon culminates in the final expression of the spirit of the bayonet—fierce and relentless destruction of the enemy. For the enemy, demoralizing fear of the bayonet is added to the destructive power of every bomb shell, bullet, and grenade which supports and precedes the bayonet attack.

For those of us training new cadets in the summer of 1969, just as when we were new cadets in the summer of 1967, this eloquent and brutal passage was summed up in a chant that was shouted across the training field, led by each squad leader and repeated by every member of every new cadet squad:

"WHAT'S THE SPIRIT OF THE BAYONET, MEN?"

"TO KILL, SIR!"

"I CAN'T HEAR YOU. WHAT'S THE SPIRIT OF THE BAYONET?"

91

"TO KILL, SIR!"

As a new cadet, I had yelled this just like the other new cadets. It was part of the ritual— you did what you were told to do without much thought or reflection. I would thrust my M 14, with the bayonet fixed on the end, forward and to the side and upwards and downwards, repeating what all the new cadets were instructed to shout about killing an imaginary enemy. Through the fatigue and frustration of Beast Barracks, bayonet drill became a rote process, one more item to endure. Now I was a leader, trying to mold young men. I had a job to do, orders to follow.

Of course, bayonet training was defensible. After all, this was the Army. It is easy to say, "That's what happens in war," or "When someone is trying to kill you, what are you supposed to do?" After all, it was an "instrumentality of accomplishing the great end of human elevation and human happiness," at least according to Senator H.V. Johnson more than 150 years ago. And admittedly, there was a sense of esprit de corps in going through the pretend violence of killing or wounding an enemy alongside your fellow new cadets. In chapel, as I mentioned before, we heard that soldiers had a great moral responsibility because they would be called upon to take another person's life. But I began to have a sense that there was no moral foundation for the bayonet drills. Wouldn't there be a greater moral responsibility to avoid taking another human's life?

So when I was required to lead bayonet training, it did not sit right with me. I had a visceral reaction to encouraging and teaching young men to mimic face-to-face killing that made me uneasy. All of a sudden, the ultimate intent of any war, killing people called the enemy, confronted me. It was not a comfortable feeling. Wasn't the sixth of the Ten Commandments "Thou shalt not kill"? Didn't Jesus teach to love your enemy? Didn't we learn in chapel to follow Jesus? All of these thoughts welled up after several sessions of bayonet drill. The only person I shared my uneasiness with was

Diane, discussing it in letters and on the phone. There was, at the time, no other outlet for discussing my feelings about bayonet training—talking about it with fellow squad leaders might have hurt my military standing when time for reviews came.

Then, in the next few weeks, I learned that one of my forty-nine high school classmates, Ralph Wellinghoff, had been killed in Vietnam on July 14, 1969. Not only did Ralph's death bring the war closer to home, it also seemed unfair. Ralph and I had not been close friends, but we lived in a town of 1,500 and were part of a small graduating class; I had known him for years. He was one of six children and had worked his ass off all the time I knew him, delivering newspapers in the morning on his bicycle. I don't recall if Ralph was drafted or volunteered for the Army, but he was one of those who had the least to gain from the Vietnam War and he lost everything.

But I guess my discomfort passed as the summer wore on, as bayonet drill gave way to conditioning marches and encouraging my squad to complete Beast Barracks and prepare to endure plebe year. Squad leaders had to make sure their squads looked good, kept their shoes and belt buckles shined, learned how to wear uniforms and make formations on time. We also had to check on their hygiene (some squad leaders asked their squad members to report, before going to bed, that they had "showered, shaved and had a proper bowel movement") and encouraged them to write home. I did not have time for reflection about the conflict between bayonet drill and theology.

On July 21, 1969, squad leaders rousted their new cadets from their bunks around midnight and marched them to Thayer Hall, where everyone was herded into classrooms. On small black-and-white TVs, we watched Neil Armstrong step off the Apollo 11 module on the surface of the moon and utter the now-famous words, "One small step for a man; one giant leap for mankind." It was a rare effort to allow new cadets access to the outside world, and I am grateful for the opportunity. I wonder how many of the exhausted new cadets remember it.

The summer was eventful in other ways. In August, I took weekend leave to be the best man at Les LeMieux's wedding to Paddy and headed south to Nyack, New York, about twentyfive miles south of West Point near the Tappan Zee Bridge over the Hudson River. There was news about an event scheduled for that same weekend, August 15–18, 1969, a couple of hours north of West Point at a little town called Woodstock. My cow-summer Beast Barracks roommate Jeff Hubsch decided to see what the publicity was about. We heard about huge traffic jams on the way to Woodstock. Jeff finally made it back just before the Sunday night curfew. He looked exhausted. He had hitchhiked up Route 9W and gotten pretty close to Woodstock. He did not make it to the actual festival and did not hear any music. One thing he did share with those who made it to the festival was getting caught in the rain. And inevitably Beast Barracks II wound down toward another Reorganization Week.

CHAPTER 11:

A NEW PRESIDENT, A NEW STRATEGY, THE SAME WAR

In January 1969, before Richard Nixon was inaugurated as President, preliminary peace negotiations were underway in Paris. These talks had nothing to do with ending the fighting. Rather they involved the shape of the table where the negotiations would occur, and even whether the government of South Vietnam would be a party to them. On March 18, the United States began to carpet bomb Cambodia. Later in 1969, President Nixon ordered 60,000 troops to be withdrawn from Vietnam, as the strategy changed to "Vietnamization," which meant making Vietnamese soldiers, rather than American GIs, responsible for the major part of the fighting. Unfortunately, the South Vietnamese government was increasingly corrupt. By the end of 1969, President Nixon said the US was looking for "peace with honor" in Vietnam.

Meanwhile, in addition to the moon landing and Woodstock, on November 15, 1969, nearly 500,000 people attended an anti-war march on Washington, D.C., in what was dubbed at the time the largest anti-war march in US history. For us back at West Point, though, cadet life went on.

Right before Reorganization Week, a major change was instituted for about 200 First Regiment cadets. As the Vietnam War dragged on, enrollment at West Point continued to increase. So, following the Army's penchant for doing things by twos, it added two companies to each regiment, H and I. I was assigned to Company H1. It was unexpected, and it meant that I had to get to know many new classmates. The positive was that Companies H1 and I1 were housed in new barracks that, on one side, looked out over the parade ground and down the Hudson River. It was a rough job for the new Company H1 cadet commander. I don't recall his name, but he did a good job. Just as in Beast Barracks, juniors were squad leaders or assistant squad leaders, with just a few exceptions. To start the year, I was named an assistant squad leader, a post without too much responsibility. I was disappointed that I had not been chosen as a squad leader, I suppose, but it left more time for academics.

After the nightmare academic schedule of yearling year, cow year seemed like it would be a piece of cake. Looking ahead, I had classes in electricity (aka juice), advanced physics 3, mechanics of solids, thermodynamics, and several social science classes. It was twenty-two hours again, but it did not seem as bad as yearling year academics.

There was still Army football, although the team's performance was less stellar than it had been the previous two years. On October 11, 1969, the Corps travelled to New York City for a game with Notre Dame. We marched into Yankee Stadium before the game and must have looked impressive in formation in our long gray overcoats. That was the high point of the game for West Point, however. Notre Dame was a powerhouse and trampled us 45–0. After that blowout, Army football was a further disappointment, ending 4–5–1. At least we shut out Navy 27–0.

My first-semester intramural sport was tennis. I was a pretty good tennis player, having played in high school, and perhaps I had improved a bit watching the great Arthur Ashe, stationed at West Point as a second lieutenant, coach the West Point tennis team during 1968. The Army tennis team practiced and played on clay courts that were right on the main road through campus, across from the library, and in the spring I would stop for a few minutes and watch him play. On October 15, 1969, I returned to my room after an intramural tennis match and was looking out over Thayer Road toward the parade ground. What I saw was another step, following on leading bayonet drill, toward the end of my West Point career.

October 15, 1969, was Moratorium Day[19], although I didn't realize it until I saw a large number of young women ready to watch the parade. They were from Vassar, I learned. Here is how the Vassar Encyclopedia describes the Vassar invasion:

"For the past week, the top officials of the U.S. Military Academy at West Point have been practicing their Military Police in riot control and the use of tear gas," an ephemeral Vassar publication, *Blood & Fire*, reported in October 1969. "Their fear: an onsurge of college girls from Vassar with anti-Vietnam War petitions in hand, and armed with facts, reason and charm." Far from an aggressive "onsurge," 200 Vassar students armed with flowers and calls for peace entered the military campus on October 15. Many cadets scoffed at the effort and spread rumors that Vassar girls were there to "offer their bodies in exchange for signatures on anti-war petitions." Army cheers drowned out Vassar freedom songs as cadets outnumbered the protestors nearly four to one. In the end, Vassar girls managed to discuss the war with some cadets but the event was largely considered to be a failure. No cadets signed antiwar petitions or acknowledged sympathy with anti-Vietnam thoughts, and the front page of the October 17

---

19 The Moratorium involved large demonstrations, teach-ins and student strikes in cities and colleges across the country.

issue of *The Miscellany News* declared: "West Point Invasion 'Fails,' Cadets Maintain Stronghold."

What I remember most is that when the West Point band played "The Star-Spangled Banner" at the end of the day's parade, the Vassar women did not stand up. This was unheard of, disrespectful and unpatriotic. I was shocked. And it started me thinking, why would someone sit during our national anthem? What I saw that Moratorium Day reopened the uncomfortable feelings that had surfaced while leading bayonet drills the past summer.

According to a *New York Times* article from November 7, 1969, the US was looking for a way out of Vietnam. One article claimed the US was not committing troops to an unending war because it wanted to see if Vietnamese troops could hold their own against North Vietnamese battalions; the paper quoted an officer as saying this was Vietnamization. Unknown to me at the time, protesters referred to this policy, accurately, as "changing the color of the corpses." [20] Another article the same day quoted American officials as saying a withdrawal from Vietnam was possible by mid-1971. But a week later, on November 15, 1969, a second moratorium drew 500,000 protesters to Washington, D.C., as well as protests in other cities.

The moratorium made me start thinking about why we really were fighting in Vietnam. Was it really necessary? But my thinking was not about politics. Over the coming months, I started thinking again about the morality of killing people in war. These were internal conversations with myself and external conversations with Diane—of course, I couldn't talk about this with my roommates at first. Also, as I said before, reflection was not encouraged, and I still had to study. I still figured that when push

---

20 58,000 US soldiers were killed in Vietnam. The United States estimates that between 100,000 and 250,000 South Vietnamese soldiers were killed in that war.

came to shove, I would finish at West Point, select a branch of the Army not as close to combat as infantry or artillery, try to qualify for graduate school right away, put in my time and resign after five years. This was in what little spare time I had. There was still homework every night. There were still parades and inspections. There was still a cadet rock band. There was electricity class and figuring out theoretical circuit calculations. There was mechanics of solids, learning about the vectors of forces. There was a class in law, which seemed to come to me naturally, unlike the engineering classes. Finally, the first semester ended with good grades, the dean's list and increasingly mixed feelings about the military and continuing at West Point.

CHAPTER 12:

WHAT NEXT?

By Christmas, I was seriously questioning whether to leave West Point, and if so, how. I spoke with my parents over Christmas vacation. I had mentioned my growing discomfort with the military in telephone conversations with them, but at home I mentioned for the first time the possibility of claiming conscientious objector status. They were, understandably, opposed. My father thought it would be a mistake given how far I had progressed at West Point. My mother did not understand how my views on the Army were changing. They both understood the religious argument, but they felt there were ways to remain at West Point and in the Army without having to deal directly with my opposition to killing. They were sure that this was a phase that would pass once I returned to the academy. They wanted me to graduate, and given their backgrounds, my dad as an army officer and my mom who had unsuccessfully volunteered for the WAVES, were hard pressed to understand how one could be a conscientious objector unless they were from a group like the Quakers. This was the first major disagreement I had ever had with my parents, and it left me very uncertain, so I threw myself back into West Point's daily grind.

Still, after Christmas, I kept coming back to Jesus' teachings, which my parents, especially my mother, had emphasized my whole life. Love your neighbor as yourself. And who is your neighbor? Whenever you have fed, clothed, or helped someone in need, you have fed, clothed or helped Jesus. Why did West Point not at least point out to cadets the moral issues in preparing for war? In hindsight, I believe that was a mistake. I looked into St. Augustine's and St. Thomas Aquinas' Just War doctrine. That doctrine, which dates to the fourth and thirteenth centuries, provides that a war first must be based on Just Authority: is a nation acting within legitimate political contours? Second, there must be Just Cause: has some wrong been committed against the nation that makes a violent response acceptable? Third, Just Intention: is the war aimed only at addressing the Just Cause, or is there "mission creep"? Fourth, is war the last resort? Have all available alternatives been exhausted? In addition, the Just War doctrine requires the degree of force to be proportional to the ends of the Just Cause, and a Just War must discriminate between combatants and non-combatants.[21] Was the Vietnam War just? Could any war be?

I also began exploring my feelings to test whether I was truly opposed to wars, if my feelings were based on a view that the Vietnam War did not meet the Just War criteria, or if I was simply wishing I had resigned when I had a chance. Was my thinking just convenient? Who was I among 4,000 cadets to question what we had all come here to learn? And what difference would it really make if I graduated but served in a non-combat role? I had heard of conscientious objectors, and I knew that Quakers did not believe in going to war, but not much else.

I also found the time to read Hermann Hesse's *Siddhartha*. The concept of humanity being connected, moving together like the river where Siddhartha ends up being a boatman, was compelling. The main road coming into West Point was Route 9W, which became Thayer Road, and

---

21 Later, I discuss how Pope Francis has called the Just War doctrine into question given the magnitude of weapons available today.

it ran between the south gate and the academic part of the base. It ran along the bluff overlooking the Hudson River. I would walk down Thayer Road toward the hotel, where I could watch the Hudson River flow past between its bluffs. Watching the river flow and swirl and move on brought home the idea from *Siddhartha* that all life, especially humanity, was connected and interdependent. It fit with Jesus' teaching to love your neighbor as yourself— which implies that you have to love yourself first. The river of humanity was made up of our neighbors. How could I love myself if I was going to be part of an organization whose mission was to kill other people if ordered to do so? I struggled to rationalize my mission as a cadet with my religious beliefs.

I obtained and read a book called *We Won't Go* about young men who had either become conscientious objectors or resisted the draft. This book was eye opening because it included personal accounts of men who had burned draft cards, refused to cooperate with the draft, unsuccessfully applied for conscientious objector status to draft boards obviously biased against anyone who did not believe in killing people and some who refused orders to board transportation to Vietnam while in the Army. I was both shaken and buoyed by the courage of these young men. I read *The Pacifist Conscience*, which contained articles about the philosophical and moral issues related to objecting to war as a solution. One article, "Letter to a Non-Commissioned Officer" by Leo Tolstoy, directly pointed out the contradiction of a soldier being ordered to war while those doing the ordering championed the Bible, which forbade not only murder but also insulting other people. I read of the Quakers, whose belief in an "inner light" led them to view war as inconsistent with Jesus' spirit. I became aware of Martin Luther King, Jr.'s commitment to nonviolence. Of course, I kept these books out of sight to avoid uncomfortable questions I was not ready to answer. I read the Bible, looking for a way to justify staying at West Point, at least partly because pacifism seemed so impractical. It was not until later that I read Joseph Heller's *Catch-22*, in which Yossarian, who wants to exit the Army Air Corps in disgust at the toll of World War II, is asked, "What if everyone believed like you do?" His response: "Then I'd be a fool to believe any different." He then sets off in a quixotic crossocean journey in a rescue raft. I realized that there are times when practicality must take a back seat to one's own deeply held beliefs.

Still, although I was thinking about conscientious objector status, I was leaning toward remaining at West Point. In retrospect, I was working through my feelings in letters home. I asked my parents in a letter, dated February 9, 1970, "Why do I (or anyone) have to serve the country by fight-ing—wouldn't it be a lot more constructive and valuable to the country for me (anyone) to work in VISTA or Head Start or the Peace Corps. ... I'm not quitting or anything— that would be worse than staying, I'm sure. This has sort of been building up, but I only realized in the last couple months how I really felt." But I also reported on my grades and that I scored eighteen points in an intramural basketball game. On February 19, 1970, I wrote to my parents, "I'm sort of stuck here, actually. The only possible way out now without going in the army is probably becoming a CO. I'm not sure I could do that. I know you strongly disapprove of them." I told them that I could most likely graduate and end up in a non-combat role, but that would sim-ply put other people into positions where they, rather than me, might cause people to be killed. I observed that pacifists may not have answers, but they did have questions that deserved to be answered. I also commented on the self-perpetuating nature of the military: "Most military people believe very strongly that they are necessary and sometimes, like in Vietnam (I think) they want to go out of their way to prove it."

On March 1, I wrote a three page single spaced letter home where I said, "I don't want to be in the army. That I know. The question arises,

'Why?' It's not easy to answer because there are so many factors which could or do enter into the 'why?' that they are almost impossible to sort out. It requires being completely honest with oneself and that is almost impossible to do; just trying is frustrating often and confusing always; at the moment I feel both frustrated and confused. Why do I even bother? It would be much simpler and less painful to just forget the whole thing and continue on as in the past, but I just can't. This is something I've got to face." In this letter, I closely questioned my motives. "Why don't I want to be in the army? Maybe it's because I don't want to be killed. Nobody does, and I'm no different in that respect than anybody else. But I've repelled off a 60-ft cliff; I've slid across a lake from 50 ft. high and a pulley and landed in the water. I've climbed a series of platforms—about 5—separated by 7 or 8 feet to the top. Surely that can't be the only reason, can it?" I offered two other reasons; first, that I didn't believe in war, and second that I did not want to kill anyone. "Cadets are taught that the mission of the infantry is to 'close with and destroy the enemy.' The spirit of the bayonet is 'to kill.' The killing radius of the 105 mm howitzer is 50 meters; the grenade launcher is only 5 meters. Do you realize how much time has been put into planning military strategy—almost all for the purpose of killing?" I concluded, how-ever, by telling my dad that I had not made up my mind about leaving and I was listening to his reasons why I should stay.

While I was working through these complicated feelings, going to class and living the daily cadet routine, I met several times with Chaplain Michael Easterling, one of West Point's assistant chaplains. Chaplain Easterling was an American Baptist pastor who had graduated from Wheaton College, an evangelical Protestant college in Wheaton, Illinois. Rev. Easterling is a member of Wheaton College's athletic hall of fame as a soccer goaltender. He was the epitome of a pastor, and I was able to dis-cuss with him the extremely difficult issues surrounding reconciling the

Bible with the Army's mission without fear that he would reveal them to my commanding officers. Among other things, he told me that I should "severely question" my motives and to be absolutely certain before I made any decision about leaving. While he and I disagreed about a number of issues, I do not recall that he ever told me that I was wrong. He pointed out that I was looking for an absolute answer, that looking for an absolute answer in the Bible is a challenge and that I needed to be very sure if I said I was opposed to war while at West Point. He warned me that if I applied to be a CO, the Army would be hard on me. I also met a few times confidentially with a counselor from the psychology department and with my law professor, who was an attorney. They all questioned me about how I arrived at my beliefs after being at West Point for three years. My law professor in particular was sympathetic because while he had been with a large New York City law firm, he strongly opposed the Vietnam War. They were good questions, and I had to wrestle with the answers. I had to be sure that I was being truthful to myself.

By March 1970, I seriously began to explore options for leaving West Point. Just the thought of explaining why I had come to believe that I could not kill other humans—in the midst of living daily in an institution where that not only was an accepted outcome but to some cadets, officers and enlisted men, a goal—was overwhelming. How could I do this, especially when there was barely time for normal duties and responsibilities? As you will see later, the Army found me to be insincere in large part for supposedly deciding in February that I was a conscientious objector, but waiting until academics were over to submit the application. But that was not the case. I was only in the first stages of exploring what it meant to be a conscientious objector, whether I met the criteria, how to go about it and what the consequences would be if I applied and failed. I knew I needed practical advice as well as spiritual guidance.

First, I called a draft counselor for Orange County, New York, the county where West Point was located. He put me in touch with Marvin Karpatkin of the American Civil Liberties Union (ACLU), who was representing Lt. Louis Font at the time. Lt. Font was a West Point graduate who was applying for discharge from the Army as what was called a "selective CO"— he did not oppose war in general but was opposed on religious grounds to the Vietnam War. He also referred me to Joan Goldberg of the law firm Rabinowitz, Boudin and Standard and the National Emergency Civil Liberties Committee (NECLC) in New York City. The NECLC had split from the ACLU in the 1950s because the ACLU would not directly defend individuals charged under the McCarran Act for advocating the overthrow of the United States government. I learned that Ms. Goldberg's firm represented clients such as Cuba, Chile under Allende, Paul Robeson and Julian Bond, and was active in the civil rights movement and representing labor unions. Given these clients, it was considered more radical than the ACLU.

The weekend of April 22, 1970 I took weekend leave and Diane and I traveled to New York City to meet with the lawyers. Other than the law professors at West Point, these were the first lawyers I had ever met. The meeting with Mr. Karpatkin was pleasant but brief. He asked if I was morally opposed just to the Vietnam War or to war in general. Once he learned I was not interested in applying for discharge as a selective CO, he said the ACLU would not represent me.

My impression was that the ACLU was interested in trying to set a legal precedent for selective COs, and my views did not match its agenda.

I then went to Ms. Goldberg's office. She was probably in her forties, warm and outgoing. The first thing she said to me was, "Tell me about yourself." It was not the kind of question I was used to, and we hit it off, although our backgrounds were very different—me a Methodist from a small Illinois town and she a Jewish woman from New York City. She and the firm agreed to represent me. I was both ecstatic and relieved. I had hope, and I had affirmation that I was not alone. After the meeting, Diane and I went to Central Park, where the first Earth Day celebration was taking place.

Through Ms. Goldberg, I learned of Army Regulation 635-20, which, to my surprise, contained a process for seeking discharge from the Army as a conscientious objector. Of course, the regulation was single spaced and about five pages long. It explained what an application for discharge had to include:

(1) General information, including name, social security number, selective service number, permanent home address, a list of all schools attended, a list and dates of all prior jobs, all former permanent addresses, parents' names and addresses, parents' religious denomination, whether applicant applied for CO status with the Selective Service System and whether the applicant is willing to serve as a CO in a civilian capacity.

(2) Religious training and beliefs, including a description of the nature of the belief that is the basis of the claim; explain how, where and from whom the applicant received the training and acquired the current belief; the name and address of the individual on whom the applicant most relies in matters relating to the claim; a statement of the circumstances in which the applicant believes in the use of force; a description of the applicant's actions that most conspicuously illustrate the consistency and depth of the applicant's religious convictions; and whether the applicant has ever publicly expressed his beliefs, and if when and where;

(3) Participation in organizations, including whether applicant has previously been a member of a military organization, church membership, the church's view of the use of force, and any civilian organizations of which the applicant has been a member; and

(4) References.

In fact, completing the application, explaining my beliefs and how they changed, was part of the process of deciding I really was a conscientious objector. After all, my parents, Chaplain Easterling and my counselor from the psychology department, Major Cortez, questioned me every step of the way, albeit in a supportive way. In other words, I had to be honest with myself—was I considering applying as a CO because I was truly morally opposed to war, or was I trying to avoid serving in the Army in general or Vietnam in particular?

Quite clearly, preparing an application for discharge was going to be a time-consuming process that required much prayer and thought. If my application was to have any chance of success, it had to be complete and persuasive and respond directly to the questions. It had to be presented in a neat package—that is, it had to be typed. There was no template to go by other than the requirements of AR 635-20. I worked on the application for weeks, mostly on weekends. I would handwrite it and take it or mail it to Diane to type at Ladycliff. The only way to make revisions was for her to mail me a draft and for me to mail it back, or to wait for a weekend when we could meet. It was a slow process. I also met and spoke more with Joan Goldberg, and she gave me advice on how to explain my beliefs in a cogent way. I had to make sure that I followed AR 635-20 to the letter. I was talking on the phone with my parents, who continued to counsel me to stay at West Point. I was writing poetry that made it into the application. I contacted people who might offer letters of support. And since I was moving toward being a conscientious objector but still not one hundred percent certain of whether I would submit the application, I had to keep up with academics so my options would be open if I decided to stay. Plus, I was simply not able to allow myself to do poorly in academics. To do so would have been dishonest, to myself, to my parents and to my professors.

During the last couple of months of spring semester, I confided in my roommates what I was doing. They were disbelieving at first, but they eventually began to understand I was sincere, if a bit weird. One even offered and then provided a letter of support, most likely at risk to his career.[22] I was exceptionally surprised and appreciative at his support.

By May, I was becoming more certain that I was going to submit the application for discharge. And the events of that month sharpened my resolve. On April 30, 1970, President Nixon had announced publicly that the war had expanded to Cambodia, even though operations and air strikes had been happening there for years. On May 1, a series of student strikes and protests began, often targeting campus ROTC buildings. On May 4, after students burned an ROTC building at Kent State in Ohio, poorly prepared National Guard troops shot and killed four students and injured ten others. In the next few days, student protests spread to nearly 700 campuses. This news made its way to West Point. Most cadets I spoke with supported the National Guard troops.

I suppose this was to be expected, but I found it disappointing that there was so little sympathy for young men and women our age who were protesting a seemingly endless war. It became clearer to me that my beliefs were separating me from my fellow cadets. Around the same time, a professor who taught American government, Captain Deagle—one of the brightest professors I had while at West Point—told our class that he

---

22 This friend went on to graduate, join the infantry and become an airborne ranger, including serving in Vietnam. He retired after twenty years as a Lieutenant Colonel, I believe.

thought the Vietnam War was likely to end in the next couple of years, and that we should volunteer for Vietnam. The reason: having combat experience on our records would be good for our military careers. He said this matter-of-factly, in an amoral manner, as if he were suggesting that getting an MBA would be helpful to succeed at a corporation. Looking back, I can see that he was giving what he thought was the best advice to young men who had chosen a military career. But back then, it seemed gratuitous to tell us that, regardless of the morality of the profession or of the Vietnam War, we should try to take part in it simply for personal gain.

In preparing the application, I had to explain what I believed and how I came to those beliefs, and I found that writing out my thoughts and feelings and beliefs was an important part of deciding to go forward. This process helped me organize my beliefs and confirmed that I was doing the right thing. I was aware that my parents were opposed and disappointed. But I was determined. What was troubling me the most then is the same thing that troubles me now. I wrote to my parents, "I'm tired of people saying one thing and doing another. I'm tired of going to church every Sunday knowing I don't practice what I believe. I'm tired of so-called Christians ignoring what Christ said or rationalizing his words into meaninglessness whenever it is convenient. . . . For me, talking isn't enough. Maybe leaving the army isn't such a big thing, but it's a start. At least I won't be a hypocrite anymore."

When my parents wrote back that I was letting them down, I responded that I was very sorry, but "you don't seem to understand what I am doing, especially Mom. You say five years in the Army would go fast and I may not even have to go to Vietnam. I agree. However, you are missing the entire point; first, by being in the Army, I would be taking part in killing others because every organization of the Army takes part in training for combat and has the mission to defeat the enemy. By being part of the Army I would be condoning something I believe is wrong. Instead of trying to stop it, I would be accepting it."

The last few weeks of the spring 1970-academic semester dragged by. The application was almost complete, but I was waiting for more promised letters of support. I was almost sure I was going to submit the application when it was done, but I suspect there was still a tiny bit of doubt. Was I really sincere? Would submitting the application be worth the consequences? As I impatiently waited for Diane to finish typing my application and for reference letters to arrive, I studied for finals. What else was I going to do? Not show up for finals? After three years, I was so conditioned to obey orders and schedules that not going was not an option. Or telling my Company Tactical Officer I was going to submit an application for discharge from the Army as a conscientious objector in a few days? I was pretty sure that he had never heard of AR 635-20 or a soldier asking for discharge as a conscientious objector. Without the application, he would probably have looked at me as if I had lost my mind.

The day after finals ended, at the beginning of graduation week, known as June Week, May 28, 1970, the application for discharge was finally done, including the last of the reference letters. All rising first classmen, including me, were scheduled to leave on the army base tour in the next day or two. I was not even sure until the very last minute, when I left my room to deliver it, that I was going to submit the application for discharge. But as Elvis sang, it was now or never. I knew that if I were going to submit the application, I had to do it before the trip left.

AR 635-20 said the application was to be submitted to the applicant's immediate unit commander. As best as I could determine, that was Major Baker, the Company I1 Tactical Officer. I made an appointment and was extremely nervous as I made my way to his office. I had never been to his office before, and I don't even recall what building it was in. I had no idea what his reaction would be. I had never spoken individually with him, and I generally had tried my best to stay away from officers.

When I arrived, he invited me into his office. My hands were literally shaking. I saluted, and as I handed him the application I said something like, "Sir, I am requesting discharge from the Army under AR 635-20 as a conscientious objector." To his credit, as I recall, he did not yell at me. He probably asked me a couple of questions, and I made clear I did not intend to accompany the rest of my classmates on the army base tour. After a few minutes, he dismissed me with a puzzled look and sent me back to my room.

I am proud of the application I handed Major Baker.[23] It started by noting that in the New Testament, we are called on to love our neighbors as ourselves: "The New Testament teaches that we should love everyone, not only those who agree with our thoughts or support our government. Thus, I have no right to take the life of any other person since he is a necessary and special part of the universe, someone whom I have a duty to love." I explained that this commandment is simply incompatible with war. While each individual is unique and should have a place in this world, the military strips away individuality in favor of blind obedience and hatred for an enemy.

The My Lai tragedy demonstrates what can happen to individuals who are constantly told that killing other human beings is laudable. The fact that these men were serving their country at the time does not justify the massacre. In "Civil Disobedience", Thoreau states "the mass of men serve the state thus, not as men mainly, but as machines, with their bodies...In most cases, there is no free exercise whatever of the judgement [sic] or of the moral sense; but they put themselves on a level with wood and

---

23 My entire application is included as Appendix 1.

earth and stones..." I cannot accept this; . . . . I noted that I was aware that pacifism was regarded as too idealistic, because to live in human society one is taught that you must accept war and violence. I countered that concern by stating my belief in the fundamental goodness of people, who are made in the image of God, are all children of God and therefore have an infinite capacity for good. Surely if humans like Handel and Picasso could compose the "Hallelujah Chorus" or create *Guernica* we have the capacity to end war.

I candidly explained that during Beast Barracks as a plebe, I was uncomfortable with bayonet training but was able to put that uneasiness aside because I regarded West Point as an ideal. I also saw that there were many ways I could contribute to the Army other than in hand-tohand combat. Additionally, "I can remember being told in chapel that a soldier has the greatest moral responsibility of any person since he must take human life. Somehow, this statement seemed wrong, because the Bible says 'Thou shalt not kill,' and 'turn the other cheek.' However, I assumed that a chaplain knew more than I did and pushed the doubts to the back of my mind." I wrote how this uneasiness stayed dormant until I was a squad leader in Beast Barracks between yearling and cow years.

This time, I was on the teaching end of the bayonet, training incoming plebes to kill people. The beauty of the river and surrounding hills stood in sharp contrast to the savage growls of the new plebes, trying to emulate the "trained killer" on the demonstration platform. I wondered how many realized what they were doing... But I couldn't dwell on such somber thoughts. I was a squad leader, with a role to play; I had to set the example for my eleven followers, and I figured that an example which rejected the goals they were trying to achieve was no example at all. Therefore, I closed my eyes to the brutality of the summer training to play the role expected of me.

Nonetheless, I wrote, I went on to read books such as "Siddhartha" and "Franny and Zooey," in which Zooey explains to his sister Franny that he pictured a lady listening to the radio on a porch, and as everywoman she was Christ herself. This description made perfect sense to me; if a lady sitting on a porch listening to the radio was the image of Christ, wasn't the same true of a Vietnamese farmer plowing his rice paddy? I related how the October 1969 moratoriums and the news of the My Lai massacre brought these feelings of uncertainty about the military back to my forefront.

At first, these ideas frightened me; they were not only unconventional, they challenged the entire meaning of something I was committed to do. Yet, to me, war was contrary to Christ's commandments. Why, then, did so many people, nominally called Christians, advocate and support wars, which are direct violation of Christ's admonition to "love the neighbor"?

I discussed this matter with Chaplain Easterling and after much prayer and thought I concluded that there is no way to reconcile the concept of loving one's neighbor and war. One question still remained. Even though no one really wants war, isn't war sometimes necessary to defend the country? I cannot answer this question for everyone; however, I cannot accept a moral code or religion, which applies one standard for individuals and another for nations and individuals acting on behalf of nations. I am willing to work for the country; on the other hand, I do not believe that killing for the defense of the country justifies the killing. On a larger scale, if the whole world realized the futility and waste of war, then there would be no need for killing.

After explaining that I had spoken numerous times with Chaplain Easterling, and having listened and prayed, I summarized my position:

> [M]y conscience calls on me to reject war as means to
> any end, and instead to substitute love. Perhaps this is not

a logical decision in the world as it is; however, I do not consider war, which involves the destruction of man and of the world given to him, a logical choice either. To me, this is the only decision I can make, given the faith I have in God and man. In addition, I believe the world can and will be made a better place than it is at present. To reject war is to place my faith in the future. For me to participate in the Army, which has as its goal the winning of wars and the destruction of life, would be to reject the better future world. I am not rejecting service to my country; however, I do not believe that one must kill to serve his country. I believe service is important and necessary, but I want to make a positive contribution, to build rather than to destroy.

These decisions have not been easy to make. My family has discouraged them, and the questions they pose have been ignored during my three years at West Point. However, in finally making them, I have been guided by the words of the Cadet Prayer: "Make us to choose the harder right instead of the easier wrong... and know no fear when truth and right are in jeopardy." For me, the harder right is to submit this request for discharge as a conscientious objector.

I concluded, "The best demonstration of the sincerity of my beliefs is the submission of this application in spite of the objections of my parents. I plan in the future to work for peace and understanding among men, to try to bring about the better world that I envision, so that someday war might become as obsolete as dueling is now."

Back in my room, I waited for the other shoe to drop. I was ordered not to go on the summer trip with my classmates, and I was moved to a section of the dorms called "boarder's ward." This was where cadets who were leaving West Point, either through resignation or by being expelled, stayed while the inevitable Army paperwork was processed. Normally, a departing cadet stayed in boarder's ward only two or three days. But I was not resigning, and I was not being expelled—at least yet. I was neither fish nor fowl, and I began what was probably the longest boarder's ward stay in West Point history.

One of the first things that Major Baker did was to contact Chaplain Easterling. On June 2, Chaplain Easterling sent back a memo attesting to having met with me a number of times during the past few months:

> I am writing in response to your recent request concerning Cadet Donham, who has recently applied as a conscientious objector.
>
> I have known Cadet Donham for one year and have talked with him on several occasions. Cadet Donham has had many questions concerning many theological and philosophical questions about killing end violence.
>
> I have attempted to answer his questions, to examine his motivations, and to offer guidance.
>
> Though we have disagreed on many issues, I believe Cadet Donham to be sincere in his convictions and to be a young man of integrity.

Another requirement of AR 635-20 was for a psychiatrist to interview the applicant. I found this ironic—a cadet willing to follow orders and kill the enemy (which, in Vietnam, too often included civilians) was perfectly sane, but a soldier who questioned the morality of his role might be deranged. This requirement also was reminiscent of "Catch 22":

> There was only one catch and that was Catch-22, which specified that a concern for one's safety in the face of dangers that were real and immediate was the process of a rational mind. Orr was crazy and could be grounded. All he had to do was ask; and as soon as he did, he would no longer be crazy and would have to fly more missions.

So, dutifully, on June 10, 1970, I had my interview with Maj. Rodger Kollmorgen, chief of neuropsychiatric service at West Point. He determined that I had no emotional disturbance or psychiatric disease, could participate in my own defense and could tell right from wrong. The psychiatrist, also an officer, reported that I was not mentally ill and that while his role was not to judge the merits of my application, my reasoning was "cogent."

The Army being involved, an officer also asked me to complete an official disposition form requesting discharge, which the Army helpfully wrote for me in bureaucratese and directed me to sign.

To Tactical Officer,

From Cdt Cary E. Donham,

Date 4 June 1970 Company I,

1st Regiment C'I0229

1. Under the provisions of AR 635-20, I request to be discharged from the Army on the grounds that I am a Conscientious Objector,

2. Pertinent information supporting this request is attached hereto,

3. I have been counseled concerning possible non-entitlement to benefits administered by the Veterans Administration due to discharge from the military service as a Conscientious Objector. I understand that a discharge as a Conscientious Objector who refuses to perform satisfactory military duty or otherwise to comply with lawful orders of competent military authority shall bar all rights based upon the period of service from which discharged, under any laws administered by the Veterans Administration except any legal entitlement (if any) to any war risk,

4. Government (converted) or National Service Life Insurance, Under the provisions of paragraph 4d, AR 635-20, I desire to have my lawyer, Joan Goldberg, appear with me before an officer in the grade of O-3 or higher, who is knowledgeable in policies and procedures relating to conscientious objector matters. 5. Under the provisions of

paragraph 6a, AR 635-29, 1 refuse to tender my resignation as a cadet pending the outcome of this request.

For the next two weeks, I languished in Boarder's Ward while my classmates were on leave or on the summer military installation trip. I hit tennis balls against a wall on the tennis courts and tried to learn how to play catch with a lacrosse stick. I also floated the idea to my folks that Diane and I were considering getting married in the fall.

On June 10, Maj. Baker forwarded my application to Brigadier General Samuel Walker, the Commandant of Cadets.[24] That was the last action any West Point officer took that displayed any meaningful effort to determine whether I actually qualified as a conscientious objector. What happened over the next three months was designed to discredit me, remove me from West Point and put me on active duty.

---

24 General Walker's son was my classmate in the First Regiment. We were acquaintances but not friends. I thought having my dad as a coach was uncomfortable. Imagine, as a cadet, having your father as the West Point Commandant of Cadets!

CHAPTER 13:

THE ARMY'S HEARING OFFICER DENIES MY APPLICATION FOR DISCHARGE

One of the key requirements of AR 635-20 was that the applicant be interviewed by an officer knowledgeable about the requirements for conscientious objector status. At first, West Point wanted to get this technicality out of the way quickly and set a June 9 date. However, I had a right to counsel, and as Ms. Goldberg was not available on June 9, the interview was set for June 16.

While waiting for the interview to take place, West Point had already decided that I did not belong there, regardless of the merits of my application. On June 11, Colonel Richard J. Tallman, the acting Commandant of Cadets while General Walker was away from the post, forwarded my application to the Superintendent, General William Knowlton. Colonel Tallman's cover memo did not give any thought to whether I, in fact, qualified for conscientious objector status. Rather, without even considering my record over three years at West Point, he immediately jumped to the conclusion that I should be discharged for lack of aptitude. I suspect that he thought if I could be expelled quickly, West Point might not have to deal with a cadet claiming CO status. There is no record of Gen. Knowlton's immediate reaction. I only learned of these actions much later through freedom of information requests.

The next day, June 12, a different colonel, Herzog, sent a memo to the superintendent's chief of staff with a similar but more cautious message: refer Cadet Donham to an aptitude board, but get approval from the Department of the Army first. Presumably, unlike Tallman, he realized that my application for discharge had the potential to be mishandled, and in the grand Army tradition, he was looking to cover his bosses' asses. That same day, another colonel sent a memo to Commandant of Cadets Gen. Walker recommending that I be referred to an aptitude board. Either the Department of the Army had responded quickly or the collective wisdom was that my exit from West Point should be expedited—but with an appearance of objectivity.

Tallman's reaction is probably understandable. Drafted in World War II and serving as a machine gunner in the Battle of the Bulge, he was awarded a field commission and attended West Point after the war, graduating in 1949. He then served in the Korean War and four tours in Vietnam. After his assignment at West Point, he was promoted to Brigadier General and returned to Vietnam, where he would be killed in action in July 1972. He was the last U.S. general officer killed in Vietnam. Despite our polar opposite views, I have no doubt that Col. Tallman honestly believed in the army's mission both at West Point and in Vietnam and was a real patriot.

The Superintendent, Maj. General William Knowlton, was a warrior, no doubt. But from my limited observation, he had no sense of humor or ability to see any perspective other than that of a single-minded, gung-ho military officer. After graduating from West Point, he served in Europe in World War II, where he was awarded a Silver Star. He then progressed through the ranks and served two tours in Vietnam as an assistant division commander and as an assistant to General Westmoreland. He oversaw one of several unsuccessful and misguided "pacification" programs aimed at gaining the confidence of rural South Vietnamese peasants. He arrived at West Point after the disgraced previous superintendent, Major General Samuel Koster, was demoted for his role in covering up the My Lai massacre. I am sure Knowlton was given the mission to regain any loss of reputation West Point may have suffered under Koster's command. As mentioned, the memo he received from Col. Tallman did not discuss whether my application for discharge was meritorious. It appeared to have a single purpose: pave the way for me to be thrown out of West Point for lack of aptitude as quickly as possible. This approach was typical of the Vietnam-era Army. Look at the immediate issue, and do not look down the road at a bigger picture. Celebrate the body count and overlook that you are killing more civilians than enemy soldiers while the people are turning against you. If something is in your way, run it over or gun it down, and ask questions later. This approach ultimately backfired in Vietnam, and I believe it backfired with me, as you will see.

The next step in what the record shows was a process with a foregone conclusion was the June 16th interview with an officer who was supposed to be knowledgeable about conscientious objector rules. By then I had been moved to East Barracks as its sole resident. The interview took place in one of the administration buildings, and I was allowed five or ten minutes to talk to Ms. Goldberg before the most important interview of my life. The interviewer was Lt. Col. Gleason, an Army personnel officer; he was a large man, somewhat intimidating physically, and he made no pretense of objectivity. Ms. Goldberg was allowed to be present during the interview and was taking notes the entire time. I was not allowed to have my application with me while I was being questioned. I don't recall if Gleason bothered to take notes, or whether he had an officer with him taking notes. If the Army had notes of the interview, it either lost or destroyed them.

Lt. Col. Gleason was not stationed at West Point but was assigned as my hearing officer by the Department of the Army. Although a law school graduate, he did not have any experience as a conscientious objector hearing officer before my hearing, and there is no record I could locate that he did any other CO hearing after mine. Gleason graduated from West Point in 1956 and served in personnel management positions in Germany and Vietnam. By 1984, he would rise to the rank of full colonel and become the director of cemeterial expenses for the Department of the Army.[25]

The interview was really an interrogation. Col. Gleason seemed intent on obtaining support for what I am confident was his preconceived notion that he would recommend that my application be denied. The interview took about an hour or an hour and a half.

Gleason repeatedly asked whether I really opposed all wars or just Vietnam. At one point, I interrupted him and reiterated that I was opposed to all wars. He asked me what I would have done during World War II when Hitler was killing six million Jewish people. Would I have allowed that? This was and is one of the most difficult questions a conscientious objector candidate is almost always asked, and Ms. Goldberg and I had discussed how I could answer it. I said I would oppose Hitler like I would oppose any injustice, but I would try to follow in Gandhi's footsteps. He also asked whether I would use any amount of force if, for example, my mother was being attacked on the street. I said I would use the minimum amount of force necessary.

In my application, I had stated that while I had not planned on selecting the infantry as a combat arm upon graduation, I had long believed I could pick a branch, such as air defense artillery or military intelligence, which had a lower chance for direct combat. This was because my class rank was high enough so that I would be able to choose whatever Army branch I wanted, and if my senior grades continued to be as good as junior year's, I might end up in the top five percent of my class academically and have a chance to go directly to graduate school or law school. Gleason seemed skeptical, even though his own service in Vietnam had been in an administrative rather than a combat role.

He asked why I submitted my application to Maj. Baker when I did, and I said I wanted to finish final exams. Gleason latched on to this answer, and he relied on it as a convenient basis for finding my application insincere: he implied if I was really sincere about being a CO and had decided in February to seek discharge, I wouldn't have continued at West Point for three more months just to get academic credits. Joan recognized that my statement about the timing of my application was unfortunate and could be misunderstood. After Gleason's questioning, we spoke for a few minutes outside the room to clarify this statement. When we went back in, Joan asked me when I finished the application, and I told her that I finished it the day before I submitted it to Maj. Baker.[26]

Only two days after the interview, Gleason submitted a memo up the chain of command that recommended that my application for discharge be denied because I was insincere. He emphasized his conclusion that I had decided to become a CO in February 1970 but managed to complete the entire semester as evidence of my alleged insincerity. That was not true, and he knew it—I told him that February was when I began to seriously consider exploring whether I was a conscientious objector, not when I had decided. I did not even meet with lawyers for another two months, in late

---

26 Joan Goldberg transcribed her notes and sent them to West Point by mail a week later, as this was well before fax or email.

April. Underlying his memo was the implication that I was lying in my application and in my statements to him. If that were true, I would have violated the Cadet Honor Code—a cadet will not lie, cheat or steal—simply by submitting my application for discharge, and he should have referred me to the Cadet Honor board to determine if I should be expelled for violating it. He didn't do that, nor did anyone else at West Point ever complain I lied in my application. And I did not lie.

The Army acted as if one day I woke up and decided I was a conscientious objector. If the Army truly believed this, it was hopelessly naïve. The Army consistently refused to understand that deciding to apply as a conscientious objector was not a decision I made in a single day, a night or even weeks. It was a lengthy and difficult process. Perhaps this was because Army officers are not trained to see gray, or if they do see gray, they are trained to act based on absolutes—take that hill; shell that village; assume everyone in a hamlet is an enemy.

Gleason's memo ignored my statement as to when I finished my application. It did not fit with his preconceived story. He did not acknowledge that I told him I had only finished my application the day before I presented it to Major Baker. He did not seem to understand that deciding to apply as a conscientious objector and preparing the application itself are so serious and life changing that the take months, not hours. Yet, he did not ask how long it took to prepare the application. He had his mind made up, and I am sure he was following orders: do not allow Donham to be discharged as a conscientious objector. He did not even discuss whether simply telling your Company Tactical Officer you were thinking about applying for discharge as a CO, without the required application, would have been a rational option.

Gleason mentioned that I had decided as early as Beast Barracks not to "go infantry" and that I had participated in the Camp Buckner training, which, as I discussed, involved training in all the combat arms and every sort of weapon generally available to soldiers in 1968. He, like many Army officers at the time, had a static view of the world and of people. He failed to acknowledge that young people in their late teens can think independently and change their attitudes and beliefs. I am sure there were many other cadets who did not plan on going into the infantry during Beast Barracks but who changed their minds over their time at West Point and became infantry officers, just as I had come to the opposite conclusion that killing people in war was immoral.

Likewise, he omitted from his memo my explanation that I was not comfortable with bayonet training in Beast Barracks but had gradually put it out of mind until my second Beast Barracks tour of duty. What I have come to realize is that during my time at West Point, I was like climate change deniers, who ignore the relatively slow pace of our changing climate, until, according to a recent United Nations report, our earth is approaching a point of no return.[27] I was indoctrinated day by day, especially with the military training being broken up by nine months of intense academics and daily life consisting of uninterrupted non-combat-related activities, so the morally difficult activities faded into the background. By the time I realized my moral earth was overheating, I was well into the second semester of junior year and had to either jump or become cooked.

Gleason claimed that I did not develop my beliefs through religious training because the Methodist Church does not take the position that its members are conscientious objectors. This turned out to be a critical mistake on his part. He did not realize that the Methodist Church supported those who served in the military as well as those who expressed faith-based opposition to war. He obviously discounted ninety percent of my application, which discussed the development of my religious beliefs in detail. In

---

27 AR6 2021: The Physical Science Basis

addition, his focus on the views of religions as a whole betrayed the fact that he did not understand the law concerning conscientious objector status, as by 1970, religious beliefs were not required to be accepted as a conscientious objector. He also ignored Chaplain Easterling's statement that he believed I was sincere, other than to say that Chaplain Easterling did not agree with my views:

> Cadet Donham claims to rely principally on the counsel and guidance of Chaplain Easterling in religious matters. He states they do not agree as to his conviction against participation in war. To rely on an individual, one indicates he relies on that man's judgement [sic] and accepts his counsel and guidance. Cadet Donham does not.[28]

In other words, Gleason did not mention Chaplain Easterling's conclusion that I was sincere and a man of integrity. To me, this omission most graphically displayed his bias and preconceived conclusion. Instead, according to Gleason, true evidence of my religious sincerity would have been for me to discard my beliefs because Chaplain Easterling and I disagreed about participation in war after hours of discussion. Gleason also said I identified no other religious person who "influenced [my] decision," conveniently ignoring the letter of support attached to my application from Rev. Carl Carter of the New Baden, Illinois, Methodist Church where I was a member.

Further, Gleason left out of his memo that the psychiatrist had stated that my beliefs were well thought out and reasoned, even though this was a mandatory part of the requirements of AR 635-20. He commented that I seemed unsure and confused in discussing some references in my application. Among other irrelevant and incorrect statements, he said that I could

---

28 Gleason memo, June 18, 1970

not recall the author of the short story "The Most Dangerous Game," that the only book I had read was "Siddhartha" and that I attributed a quote to Tolstoy that he thought was from Thoreau. His memo used these as examples of why I was insincere, even though he himself was mistaken about the Tolstoy quote. I surely was nervous, and I did not have my application with me, although he did. I was in the most important interview of my life and I was pushing back against the entire Army establishment. Gleason clearly was trying to ambush me. I suspect, though, that he was at least as nervous as me.

Gleason noted, accurately, that in high school I had participated in the Civil Air Patrol and that at Camp Buckner I had completed RECONDO training and had taken part in hand-to-hand combat training. He questioned my application because I had mentioned that in considering whether to apply as a CO, I recognized I would have the ability to select one of the combat arms less likely to see front line combat. This option, however, was true of any cadet who had earned a high enough class rank, as I had done. He concluded that my application for discharge represented an attempt to avoid combat and was not sincere. Therefore, he recommended that it be denied.

There are several ironies in Gleason's recommendation. First, of the class of 1970, more than fifty graduates selected Air Defense Artillery, and more than a dozen others selected a noncombat arm such as the adjutant general corps. Was any graduate who did not select infantry, artillery or armor trying to avoid combat? If so, why were graduates allowed to select and train in those groups? I was being penalized because I had worked my ass off to be in the top ten percent of my class so I had that choice.

Second, Gleason, being selected as per AR 635-20 and being a lawyer, presumably knew that a document as serious as an application for discharge as a CO at West Point had to follow AR 635-20 to the letter. Had

I waltzed into Maj. Baker's office in February and announced, "Sir, I am applying for discharge from the Army as a conscientious objector," without the paperwork the Army required, I would have been expelled quickly, without even a hearing because I had not followed the regulations.

Third, there was no military training going on during the academic year, other than the regimentation in terms of parades, formations and strict dorm life rules. After nearly three years, those were routine, and most cadets grudgingly accepted them. Unlike the Army base tour that would follow junior year, they were minor annoyances, as they had been for the last two or three months while I was working on the application.

Fourth, as I mentioned above, Gleason's recommendation was illogical in several ways: his gratuitous and incorrect statement that I had misquoted Tolstoy; his assertion that if Chaplain Easterling had truly been my advisor, I would have changed my views to match his; his failure to acknowledge the letter from my hometown pastor; his implication that the Civil Air Patrol, a civilian organization akin to Boy and Girl Scouts, was a quasi-military organization; and the idea that to avoid the frontlines I would give up a guaranteed ability to enter a "non-combat" combat arm as a second lieutenant and West Point graduate, for the uncertainty of being tagged as a coward and possibly assigned to the Army as a specialist 4th class, with a target on my back and Vietnam as the bull's eye.

It is true that I was tripped up when Gleason asked me why I submitted my application on May 28. My quick answer was, "I wanted to finish the academic year," which became the basis for the Army denying my application. The real answer was far more complicated. Gleason, had he been fair, should have observed that months of thought and preparation went into the application. Unfortunately, he paid no attention to my attempt to explain this.

Through a Freedom of Information Act (FOIA) request to the National Archives that I submitted in September of 2019, I learned that West Point told Gleason in no uncertain terms not to allow me to supplement my position. Gleason wrote a memo on June 20, 1970, to the Commandant of Cadets transmitting his recommendation. It included the following:

> I have been further advised that this headquarters should not permit Cadet Donham or his counsel to add anything to the file. Examples of items he may desire to add are:
>
> a.   A rebuttal.
>
> b.   A brief.
>
> c.   Supplemental data to support application.

In other words, the senior Army brass, to whom Gleason reported, was not taking any chances when it came to me clarifying the (unrecorded) statements I made to Gleason.

On June 22, 1970, Major James Altmeyer, on behalf of the Commandant of Cadets, sent a memo to General Knowlton with Gleason's recommendation, concurring with Gleason's view that my application should be denied and asserting that I should be dismissed from West Point and ordered to serve three years in the Army as an enlisted person. He also noted that I had been provided with a copy of Gleason's recommendation.[29] Knowlton accepted the recommendation without any questions. However, West Point, being part of the Army bureaucracy and with everyone looking to cover their respective asses, had to forward the recommendation to the Department of the Army for final approval.

---

29 Altmeyer resigned from the Army by 1973 and became the director of a funeral home in South Carolina.

The Army's instruction to Gleason to not allow any supplement to his recommendation was prescient. On June 23, 1970, Joan Goldberg mailed her 20-page transcription of the interview to Gleason, which showed that his recommendation was materially inaccurate and incomplete. Joan's letter enclosing the transcription was certainly timely. We were not told that Gleason would rush through a recommendation in fewer than five days and were not told that the Army would not consider any follow up information from us. In addition, his recommendation had already been forwarded to the Department of the Army before Joan's snail mail letter was delivered sometime after its mailing date of June 23. It is not clear whether the Army ever considered this important document because the Superintendent had ordered Gleason not to allow me to supplement the record, although Joan's letter may have been forwarded to the Department of the Army several weeks after Gleason's recommendation

During June, as I mentioned, I was the sole resident of East Barracks, where more than 400 cadets lived during the academic year. An internal memo to the Superintendent warned that I should have "minimal contact" with Beast Barracks, which would start the first week of July. I assumed I had permission to go down to the East Barracks basement in the evening, where the phones were, but I never knew for sure. I called Diane on the basement pay phones most evenings anyway. There were no computers and no email, just snail mail. I could read and listen to records in the evening. That was it. For the most part, I was left alone after dinner.

To solve the problem of what to do with me during working hours, the Commandant assigned me to work in the West Point base mail room. Not far from the mess hall in the center of the cadet barracks, about three-quarters of a mile from East Barracks, was a small yellow brick administration building where enlisted men sorted mail. During the summer of 1970, there were two enlisted men—call them George and Jerry—sorting mail, along with me. Jerry and George had been drafted, were in for two years and were grateful to have ended up at West Point sorting mail, rather than sorting dead soldiers in Vietnam at Hamburger Hill near Hue, where forty-six men of the 101st Airborne Division of the Army had been killed in May. George had a master's degree in history from an Arizona university and was, to say the least, disenchanted with the Army. The first day I met him, he told me almost gleefully that he was "short," meaning he only had three months to go before he was out, and with three months, he was likely to stay at West Point sorting mail. Jerry, who was married and from New Jersey, still had more than a year to go and hoped if he just lay low he would spend it right where he was: fifty miles from the Jersey Shore where he grew up. Draftees like George and Jerry were, as far as I could tell, invisible to the officers who ran the corps of cadets and to the cadets themselves. The Superintendent, the Commandant and their staffs did not even consider how my working eight hours a day with draftees might further reinforce my opposition to war. But it did.

At the end of June, I was allowed to go on my summer leave. I went home to New Baden for a short time and then spent most of that month-long leave with Diane's family in Rochester. While home, over my mother's objections, I bought a small engagement ring. She, quite correctly as it turned out, thought I was rushing into this relationship. I paid no attention, of course. I proposed, offered Diane the ring, and she accepted. The time on leave was too short.

During my leave, on July 21, Lt. Col. DeLuca, one of the Commandant's staff officers, handwrote a memo to Commandant Walker telling him that he expected a decision on my application from the Department of the Army the next day. He discussed how West Point should handle my case if my application for discharge was denied but a court entered an injunction against enforcement of the Army's decision. He recommended that for the time being, I continue in the mail room and have "minimal contact" with new cadets. His memo said that if my case dragged into the academic year, I should follow my "routine," but what that meant is not clear. [30]

DeLuca, in addition to being a war hero, proved clairvoyant. The next day a telegram from the Department of the Army arrived at West Point with the terse message that the Army had denied my application because I lacked the depth of sincerity needed to qualify as a conscientious objector under AR 635-20. A few days later, a single-page form dated July 24, 1970, arrived at West Point, with a box checked noting that my application was denied and repeating at the bottom of this official decision that I lacked the required depth of sincerity. My lawyer and I found this choice of words to be frustrating. The Army did not say I was insincere, only that I lacked the required "depth of sincerity." But how did they judge my "depth of sincerity?" It was not like doing a sounding to see how deep a lake or river is. There was no dipstick the Army could have used to check whether my sincerity was a quart low. The bottom line, however: my application was officially denied. And the decision did not discuss my application, my letters of recommendation, the chaplain's and psychiatrist's reports or even Gleason's report. It was a single sentence on a bureaucratic form. Its message was "Go away, and don't bother us."

---

30 As I recall, DeLuca was fair in dealing with me even as he pressed West Point's case against me. He had been awarded the Silver Star for valor during a firefight on February 1, 1968, during the Tet Offensive. He also was involved in obtaining a Silver Star for Capt. Eddie Reed, one of his company commanders during that firefight, presented to Captain Reed's wife posthumously.

CHAPTER 14

THE APTITUDE BOARD HEARING

In 1966, West Point published a pamphlet called "An Introduction to Aptitude for the Service" and distributed it to cadets' parents. The pamphlet identified three objectives of the Aptitude system: (1) to determine cadets with outstanding leadership ability; (2) to identify cadets who are weak in leadership ability with a view toward improvement; and (3) to remove cadets who, "after receiving assistance over a reasonable period of time," can't meet West Point's standards. The pamphlet concludes, "Separations under the Aptitude System are necessary not only to prevent the commissioning of inferior officer material, but also to protect the cadet from entering a career for which he is not qualified or in which he would be neither successful nor happy." No doubt, I would not have been successful or happy in the Army, based on my beliefs. But if I were to be discharged based on lack of aptitude, I would be assigned to active duty as a specialist 4th class, exactly the opposite of what I was trying to achieve as a conscientious objector. In truth, the Army only cared about whether an *officer* might be happy or successful in an Army career—enlisted personnel were, as they have always been, little more than cannon fodder.

I returned from leave at the end of July and then learned that the Army had denied my application for discharge. I went back to my East

Barracks room and my mail room job but also found that West Point had
cleared the decks for the aptitude board Col. Tallman had recommended
shortly after I submitted my application. Aptitude boards were generally
reserved for cadets who were consistently deficient in military aptitude
under West Point's ratings, which was not me. I was somewhere in the
middle of my class in military aptitude. Nonetheless, on July 30, I received
a memo from Col. DeLuca telling me that West Point had scheduled my
aptitude board for August 6 and that I needed to provide the names of
witnesses I wanted to call by August 5. I submitted a handwritten list,
although some of the cadets I asked to call were away from West Point on
the summer tour, and West Point clearly wanted to get this hearing, essentially a formality, over. I asked for Lt. Col. Johns, who had been a psychology instructor; Maj. Baker,[31] the Company H1 tactical officer; Chaplain
Easterling; and my former roommates Michael Liberty, Michael Carver,
and Les LeMieux. My two most recent roommates, who best knew my
application process, were away from West Point for the summer, not that
their presence would have made any difference.

The Aptitude Board was a formal proceeding that again took place
in the administration building. The Board consisted of five officers, none
of whom I had had any contact with, selected from a list of about 100 officers eligible to conduct hearings. The chair was Col. Richard L. Gruenther,
who at the time was the head of the Department of Military Instruction at
West Point. My attorney accompanied me to the hearing, but she was not
allowed in the room where the hearing took place, although the chair at
first told me I could leave the room at any time to consult with her.

Col. Gruenther set the tone for the hearing by reading a prepared
statement, in which he announced that the Aptitude Board was to determine

---

31 While I had little personal interaction with Major Baker, as the company Tactical Officer
who reviewed annual military aptitude ratings, he knew that I was in the middle half of my
class in aptitude—not a rank that would normally lead to a cadet aptitude board.

whether it should recommend to the Commandant of Cadets that I should be found deficient or proficient in aptitude. He said that the board would consider how my application for discharge affected my military aptitude. While the board members had read my application, the board would not concern itself with the status of my application. Nor would it "delve into the reasons for those stated beliefs nor will we be concerned with the sincerity or insincerity of those beliefs."

Col. Gruenther then asked me three "standard" questions about whether I believed the hearing would be fair and impartial or was influenced by racial or religious prejudice and whether I wanted a career as a commissioned officer. I said I would deal with these questions in my prepared statement. I told the Aptitude Board:

> I am a conscientious objector to war—I cannot in conscience participate in war in any form. Because of my beliefs, which are based on my religious background and training, I found it increasingly difficult to participate in the military activities that are part of training at West Point.
>
> When these beliefs became so strong that further participation in the military caused great conflict within me, I sought counseling at West Point—to try to understand and accept that my belief in God and my duty to serve my country are not incompatible.
>
> During this period, I was rated for aptitude by my classmates and my superior officers. My academic standing is excellent; I stand in the middle of my class in military aptitude. . . . I believe that on the basis of my aptitude record, I must be found proficient.

I pointed out that the law and the Army recognized conscientious objector status and listed several reasons why the Aptitude Board hearing was unfair, including that I had been told before the hearing the predetermined outcome: I would be found deficient in aptitude. I was not allowed to be represented by counsel at the hearing. I did not have adequate time to locate witnesses because only about half of my classmates were present at West Point due to the first-class summer trip, and the hearing was not based on my aptitude as typically measured at West Point.

I also told the board that Lt. Col. DeLuca had told me that my conscientious objection application would not be an issue in the hearing. Gruenther immediately said he would call DeLuca as a witness. While I accurately reported what Lt. Col. DeLuca had told me, and Col. Gunether had said the same thing in his opening statement, it was clearly a lie, because my application was the only reason for the aptitude board. I also said that the Commandant of Cadets had told me a week ago that I would be found deficient in aptitude. Clearly not willing to bother the Commandant on the spur of the moment, Col. Gruenther asked the other members of the board if they had received any such instruction. They each answered they had not. This was clear nonsense. The documentary record I obtained through Freedom of Information requests shows that West Point had planned to discharge me based on aptitude ever since I filed my application for discharge, and the Board members knew to do what the Army expected.

I pointed out that my hearing was not convened based on proper regulations and cited the various criteria normally used for referring cadets to the Aptitude Board. The board admitted that my case was not "normal" based on standard aptitude ratings but was based on my unwillingness to assume the duties of an officer in the Regular Army.

The board asked me whether I had considered resigning as a cadet. I told them I had not because the real issue was not whether I should resign.

Rather, the issue was whether I should be discharged as a conscientious objector. I also said that I was willing to do three years of alternative service to fulfill my commitment.

Contrary to what Lt. Col. DeLuca had told me and to Col. Gruenther's opening remarks, they asked about the timing of my application for discharge. I explained that while I had started thinking whether I was a conscientious objector in February, when I reached out to the draft counselor, I did not consider myself to be a conscientious objector until May 28, when I submitted my application. I told them there was not a conscious connection between my application and May 28 being the date final exams ended for the spring semester.

Gruenther handed me a copy of the Oath of Office taken by commissioned officers and asked me if I could sign it. I questioned what the term "defend" meant in the oath, and suggested that it could easily refer to alternative service under existing Selective Service policies.

Gruenther thought for a minute and then said in the oath it meant what was expected of West Point graduates. I was allowed to leave the room for a short time to consult with Joan. When I returned, I declined to answer the question, claiming that to do so would be considered an unconstitutional "bill of attainder."[32] I was also told I would not be allowed to consult with counsel any more during the hearing, except to take three minutes to tell Joan of that decision. This was contrary to what the Board had originally said, when it put no limits on my leaving the room to consult with Joan.

---

32 A bill of attainder is a legislative act that singles out someone for punishment without a trial. My reference to the question involving a bill of attainder was probably incorrect, but the board didn't know either.

Gruenther then asked if I could, in my present state of mind, sign the Oath of Office now. I replied that I could not, emphasizing that it was not because I was incapable of leadership but because of my personal beliefs.

Next, the Board asked me to assume that the Army was still engaged in combat operations when I was to graduate. They asked if I would have any mental reservations about participating as a commissioned officer in such operations. I told them that I thought my previous testimony had already answered that question. They did not follow up.

They also asked me why I was wearing insignia of a junior (second classman). I said I had not performed any duties of a first classman, being assigned to the mailroom. I said that if the case wasn't resolved by the beginning of classes, I might begin classes as a first classman, but that I did not expect that to be the case.

The Board called Lt. Col. DeLuca to testify concerning my statement that my application for discharge would not be an issue. DeLuca said that what he meant was that the board would not consider the merits of my application, but it would consider the statement I made in the application in assessing my aptitude for the service. I asked him how many cadets in the middle half to their class in aptitude had been called before an aptitude board. DeLuca did not know, so I asked him if it were possible for him to find out. Before he could answer, Gruenther cut him off and said that the question was not "germane" to the issue before the board, and that there was no need for DeLuca to research that question. Gruenther then said that the record should reflect that the reason for convening the board was not my application for discharge but statements made in the application that I did not want to be part of an organization that "not only condones but glorifies war." As I reflect, that statement was intellectually dishonest because it completely ignored why I had made that statement in my application: my religious beliefs. It showed that West Point had no interest in whether I was sincere in my beliefs once the Army had ruled that I lacked the "depth of sincerity" required for conscientious objector status.

Two other officers testified. Lt. Col. Johns had been my psychology professor (and had given me an A). He opined that my application made me deficient in aptitude, and testified that he had read my application and that I was sincere in my belief that I was a conscientious objector. Hedging his bets, he then said he did not know if my beliefs were sincere. Apparently, he was not troubled that these two statements were logically inconsistent. But he knew who buttered his bread.

Major Baker, Company H1's tactical officer, testified that he had considered me proficient in aptitude until I submitted my application for discharge. He said I had never mentioned resigning as a cadet. He did not recommend that an aptitude board be convened when I submitted my application for discharge because he did not consider himself to be qualified to make that decision, but he now recommended that I be discharged from the academy.

Mike Liberty had been one of my roommates in Company H1 the first semester of junior year. Mike was an outstanding student and was in the top quarter in military aptitude. As I recall, he was extremely serious. He said when rating aptitude, he considered performance, competitiveness against academy standards and other cadets and personal appearance. He had rated me in the middle half. He had not ever heard of a cadet in the middle half in aptitude being brought before an aptitude board. Such a proceeding was reserved for cadets who were inept. He said I had the ability to be an officer but chose not to use it. He believed I was sincere. He did not recommend that I be discharged from the military academy. Rather I should not be required to go on active duty in the Army at all, even as an enlisted man, although that would be the usual path for a cadet who resigned after junior year.

Next, Cadet Michael Carver testified. He had been my assistant squad leader the last part of junior year. Michael was extremely nice and very competent. He was also nervous. He had not read my application, but I had explained to him that I held human life to be sacred, regardless of nationality, and that I could not reconcile war with God's command to love our neighbor. He rated me as in the upper middle half of my class in aptitude and my performance as a squad leader as average, based on ability to perform as a cadet and desire to perform as a cadet. Given my beliefs, he could not consider me proficient, but would not commit to recommending me for separation. He said that I was honest and sincere and should be discharged from the service if I met the criteria for discharge, but he was unfamiliar with those standards.

My former roommate and friend Les LeMieux, who had resigned as a cadet after sophomore year, spoke after Cadet Carver. Les had rated me twice in the upper quarter in aptitude and twice in the middle half in aptitude while he was a cadet. He had testified at three aptitude boards while a cadet, and each time the cadet had a poor attitude. Les said that my application for discharge should be granted because I was sincere in my beliefs. He agreed that I did not belong at West Point, not because of physical or mental ability but because of my moral beliefs. He also said that since I was not morally capable of being an officer I was not morally capable of being an enlisted man.

My final witness was Chaplain Easterling. Chaplain Easterling had known me for about a year, during which time he had had several discussions, and many disagreements, with me. He noted that while he was only generally familiar with the Army regulation on conscientious objection, he felt that I should be discharged as a conscientious objector. He believed that although I was capable of leading men in battle, as a conscientious objector I would have trouble doing so. Chaplain Easterling would not comment on my aptitude, instead stating that he supported my request for conscientious objector status. Much later, I learned that Chaplain Easterling's support for my application for discharge put his status as a West Point chaplain in jeopardy but that, due to the support of the senior chaplain, he kept his post. Chaplain Easterling proved to be a true faith leader, which became even more evident when as pastor of Madison Ave. Baptist Church in New York City, he opened the church to gays and lesbians.

The Board issued two reports of the hearing, one on August 10 and one on August 14. The August 10 report, directed to the Commandant of Cadets, said I claimed that I was not receiving fair treatment because West Point did not believe I was sincere when it considered my application for discharge, but now considered my application to be sincere when West Point wanted to discharge me. It reported that I admitted I did not seek a career as a military officer because I should be discharged as a conscientious objector. The report concluded that because I could not, due to my "recently professed beliefs," take the officer's oath of office, I should be discharged from West Point for lack of aptitude. It also stated that there was no need for a legal brief to be submitted by my counsel because my counsel was not present at the proceedings and would thus be unfamiliar with what occurred. This was disingenuous if not outright false. My counsel was present but only was not included in the hearing due to Col. Gruenther, who changed the rules in the middle of the hearing and would not even allow me to leave the room to consult with her. This also assumed that I could not report what had occurred at the hearing to my counsel. This report, which was the only one signed by all five members of the board, did not mention the witnesses' testimony.

The second report was dated August 14 and contained several revisions. First, it said that while the two officers I called as witnesses testified I should be discharged for lack of aptitude, "the other witnesses were unable to grasp the pertinence of aptitude in this situation and preferred to hedge on their recommendation of proficiency or deficiency." This was an odd comment since the witnesses included two current first classmen and one former cadet, all of whom clearly understood what aptitude meant. Unlike the August 10 report, this report omitted my statements that I did not perceive the hearing to be fair and that I believed the hearing to be the result of prejudice against my religious beliefs. Instead, it emphasized that I could not sign the oath of office, which was true, and that I intended to begin classes in the fall as a first classman, which was not true. It included one-line summaries of witness testimony, several of which were out of context and thus also misleading. For example, the report stated that Mike Liberty said only that I "had ability but choose not to use it." While this is accurate, he also said I should not be in the service at all because he believed I was sincere and that he had never heard of a cadet in the middle half in aptitude being called before an aptitude board. The report described Mike Carver as saying I could not be considered proficient in aptitude because I had no desire to be a cadet, that he believed me to be "honest and sincere," and that I should be discharged as a conscientious objector if I met the criteria. The misrepresentation of Les LeMieux's testimony was especially egregious. The report stated that Les, who had been my roommate and had known me longer than any of the other witnesses, said I should be separated, not because I lacked physical and mental ability but because I lacked "moral ability." Les clearly meant that because of my moral and religious opposition to war, it would not be fair to require me to serve either as an officer or an enlisted person, because other than status, there is no principled distinction between what an officer or enlisted person may be required to do in war. Finally, the report described Chaplain Easterling as saying that while I had ability, I would choose not to lead men in battle. This terse sentence had ignored that Chaplain Easterling said that he believed I was sincere and should be discharged as a conscientious objector. The reason I would choose not to lead men in battle was due to my religious beliefs.

Comparing the summary of the testimony with the report confirms that the aptitude board hearing was akin to a star chamber.[33] Everyone at the hearing, including the officers who made up the board and were presumably not stupid, knew the issue was my application for discharge as a conscientious objector and nothing else. Unlike Col. Gleason, whose report was based on his own unrecorded recollection of an hour-and-a-half interview (with instructions from superiors not to allow any follow-up evidence or argument), the aptitude board included statements from two current classmates and a former roommate, all of whom said I was sincere in my beliefs. Plus, Chaplain Easterling's testimony was unequivocal: my beliefs were sincere. The aptitude board was another example of a Catch 22; my application for discharge was denied because I wasn't sincere, but it was sincere enough that simply by submitting it, I lacked aptitude to be a cadet.

Who was the better judge of my sincerity? A Lt. Colonel who had never met me until he was ordered to interview me, and undoubtedly was under pressure from his superiors? A nameless Department of the Army official who relied on Gleason's misleading report? Or people who actually had lived and worked with me, and a Chaplain who had taken the time to discuss a serious moral and theological topic with a young cadet? Clearly, after the hearing, West Point could have sent the testimony to the Department of the Army and asked it to reconsider the denial of my application. It did not do that, and the months that followed were challenging not only for me but also for the Army. It had acted tactically but not strategically.

---

33 "Star Chamber," named for a secretive English body in the fifteenth to seventeenth centuries, is now a metaphor for legal or administrative proceedings with no due process rights.

West Point still does not brook any suggestion of disloyalty. In 2019, sixteen Black female seniors posed for photos in a pre-graduation event, celebrating with raised fists. While they said it was not a political statement, West Point, while allowing them to graduate, nonetheless required them to appear for counseling with the Commandant of Cadets prior to graduation. I guess it was not taking any chances. Ironically, later in 2019, West Point quickly cleared three cadets who displayed what appeared to be a white power symbol during the Army– Navy game because they claimed it was simply an innocent game. There is no record, however, of them receiving any kind of discipline.

CHAPTER 15:

WE GO TO COURT

In the meantime, on August 5, my attorneys had filed a petition for habeas corpus in the federal court for the Southern District of New York asking the court to order the Army to approve my application for discharge and release me from the service. They had also asked the court to stay my aptitude board hearing, but West Point went ahead with it after our papers were filed with the court. The odd caption of the case was *United States ex rel. Donham v. Resor.*[34]

While you might think of habeas corpus as relating to a criminal case, Joan explained to me that the Latin term means, literally, "have the body," and she wanted my body out of the Army. The petition was a public record, and it only took Craig Whitney, a young *New York Times* reporter, a few hours to find it and write a story that made it onto the front page of the Times on August 6—the same day as my aptitude board hearing. I assume that the aptitude board members knew of the article at the time of the hearing, since I did, and were not happy.

---

34 The form of caption, common in conscientious objector cases, says that Donham is filing the lawsuit to uphold United States laws. The defendant, Stanley Resor, was at that time the Secretary of the Army, and he was violating the law by denying my application for discharge.

The article noted that I was the first West Point cadet to file an application for discharge as a conscientious objector and that my lawsuit challenged the Army's denial of my application. Mr. Whitney reported that the Army had denied my request because I lacked the depth of sincerity the Army required for approval and quoted Gleason's conclusion that I would not have submitted my application if the Vietnam War had ended because I was only concerned for my personal welfare. Mr. Whitney countered Gleason's statement with part of my roommate Eric Sundin's letter of support: "Some people may say that Cary is a coward and is afraid to fight or be near danger in the Army, but I know that he has not become a conscientious objector for these reasons." While West Point declined to comment, the article closed by noting Chaplain Easterling's support. It also quoted my statement in the court papers and application that "I cannot be part of an organization which not only condones but also glorifies war and killing at the expense of both the teachings of Jesus and each man's individual humanity."

That article was quickly picked up by other newspapers and media. TV cameras and reporters showed up at my parents' house in New Baden. Joan Goldberg wanted me to have a press conference, wearing my cadet uniform, but it would have to be in New York City. As technically an upperclassman with no weekend duties, I was eligible for weekend leave, so I submitted my application. The result: I was ordered to report to the Commandant of Cadets, General Walker. He said he understood that I was involved with "some rather unsavory New York lawyers," and that he could put me in touch with some JAG (Army) lawyers who would help me out instead. He told me he was giving me the same advice he would give his own son, my classmate, and no doubt that was true. He also told me I was being used and that "he was concerned about my welfare." He asked what my plans were for the leave, and if I was going to meet with the press. I told him that was likely. He said he would prefer that I not wear my uniform. I asked him if he was ordering me not to wear my uniform while on leave, which would have been unusual. He thought for a second, and then said no and dismissed me. Despite his obvious misgivings, my leave was approved.

I took a bus to New York City and met Joan in a conference room at her law firm. I wore my summer uniform: gray trousers with a black stripe, a white short-sleeved shirt with gray epaulets and a name tag. I sat at the end of a long table, with Joan next to me and the rest of the chairs filled with reporters, along with photographers and TV cameras. They asked questions for what seemed to be a long time, and then we were done. I don't remember a single question or answer, and while I understand that a clip played on many TV stations, I never saw it and have been unable to obtain a copy from local broadcasters. However, there was a follow-up article in *The New York Times*, and press coverage spread across the country. The conservative *New York Daily News* was the counter to the favorable coverage I received from the *Times* and generally was critical of my decision.

The reporting on my application had a major impact on my family. St. Louis news stations traveled the thirty miles to New Baden and interviewed my parents. Even though they disagreed with my decision, they told the media they supported me. They eventually became ardent opponents of the Vietnam War. Some of my father's acquaintances, including church members, would not speak to him for years after my application for discharge. Ironically, that same summer, my brother Mark was applying to college, and he received calls from West Point urging him to apply to be a cadet. Apparently, the admissions office and the Commandant's office were not communicating. Mark ignored these calls and accepted a tennis scholarship to Western Illinois University. Years later during my son's high school junior year, he received emails from West Point encouraging him to apply there, which our family found amusing.

Shortly after the initial article and the news conference, my mail room work became more interesting because I started receiving letters from all over the country either praising me for my actions or calling me a traitor, a coward or worse—about seventy in all. They were handwritten and typed, addressed to Cadet Cary E. Donham, West Point, N.Y. I still have them. About two-thirds were favorable. They created lively conversation in the mail room, where pretty boring and mindless work generally dwelled.

From New York City: "Your stand is, as I am concerned, as wise and Christian as it must be difficult." From Queens, New York: "May God bless you with a good, clear heart, always, and give you courage to carry on." From New Haven, Connecticut: "We just wanted to write our support of your position and hope the best for you." From Claremont, California: "My husband and I want you to know that we support you in your statement of conscience." From a Marine lieutenant in the Concerned Officers Movement: "Is there any way we can help? Right on!" From a lieutenant in Vietnam: "You've got brothers from Woo Poo who are behind you, some in and out of the academy, that aren't saying anything—but they're behind you all the way." From a Navy Reserve lieutenant in upstate New York: "Congratulations on your outstanding and courageous stand. Do not retreat one inch." From a former West Point cadet in Virginia: "I read of your request for discharge from the Academy as a Conscientious Objector. I should like to say that I support you in your decision." There was even a letter of support from Great Britain.

On the other hand, there were those with the opposite view. From New York City: "I think you are a cheap miserable coward." From Tampa, Florida: "You are a pretty sorry specimen of a young man." From Durant, Oklahoma: "I have seen your picture in the paper and the story concerning your request for conscientious objector status at West Point. I am thoroughly disgusted!" One correspondent stands out to this day. He sent a number of anonymous envelopes (no return address) filled with clippings from *The New York Times* and the *New York Daily News* with anti-Semitic messages scrawled in the margins: "Why a Jew to defend you?" "They are masters of deceit." "99.4% of communists are Jews." This was my introduction to anti-Semitism, and it was truly shocking. It also displayed the real cowardice of people with hateful views—they did not dare to identify themselves.

The supportive letters meant a lot to me. They let me know that I was not crazy in opposing war and standing up to the military. They let me know that there were Christians who had the same feeling about war as I did. They showed me that even in the military there were soldiers who supported what I did. They also demonstrated the reach of the media even back in 1970: a couple of articles in The New York Times and a single press conference traveled from New York to St. Louis to Oklahoma to California in two or three days. The news even made it to Danville, Illinois, where my Aunt Margaret saw the press conference on a Peoria TV station and wrote my mom that she thought I explained my position well.

I wonder what kind of media response there might have been today, in the age of social media and twenty-four-hour TV and radio news. I doubt that I would have received the personal expressions both of support and opposition today from people who took the time to write or type a physical letter, sign their name, address and envelope and mail it to West Point, New York, trusting that it would reach me. But they might have posted on Twitter or Facebook.

When I returned to West Point after the news conference, the officers retaliated by getting stricter with me. First, they made sure I got up at 6:15am. Then, they ordered me to get a haircut. I wrote home, "They are so stupid; they know they are going to kick me out in a week or two, but they have to feel important, so they make you do stuff. I guess they think they're hurting me—rather, keeping me in my place. I don't understand so many of these officers."

Unfortunately, my lawsuit was not going so well. The judge had declined to stay my aptitude board hearing, which had occurred anyway by that time. He did say, thankfully, that the Army could not expel me based on lack of aptitude while he considered my lawsuit. The United States Attorney weighed in on the side of the Army and argued that the Army's decision to deny my application should be upheld. As August waned, my options were closing. I was accomplishing nothing hanging on at West Point. I could not start classes given my situation. I was truly in limbo. After all my hard work for three years to make it to the top ten percent of my class academically, I did not want to be expelled. I could resign as a cadet, but that would mean I would receive orders to report somewhere as an enlisted man, specialist 4th class, with a threeyear commitment. I always knew this was a possibility, but it was especially stark to face it head on. We finally worked out an arrangement whereby I would go on unpaid leave pending the outcome of my lawsuit. So, on August 25, 1970, I left West Point, three years and fifty days from the morning I met the man in the red sash.

On my way out, I was ordered to the office of the Superintendent, General Knowlton. I must have been wearing a uniform. He was 'generaled' up, with a freshly pressed khaki uniform and rows of ribbons. I reported and saluted. He told me I was a disgrace to the Corps and had dishonored the uniform. I tried to explain that I had not said anything negative about West Point and that I had asked General Walker if I was being ordered to not wear my uniform to the press conference. He interrupted, scowling: "Silence. Get out of here, and I never want to see you again." I concluded that he did not like me. The feeling was mutual. He clearly did not take me seriously. He was a bully, relying on his high rank to berate a young man he considered inferior, without giving the least thought to what I said. I expected more from a man who had reached such an esteemed position.

The next few days are very hazy. What was I going to do? Where was I going to live? In another twist of fate, I went from West Point directly to the heart of Greenwich Village. Joan put me in touch with a seventeen-year-old high school dropout, Jon Gottlieb, who was living in a sixth-floor walkup studio apartment at 91 Christopher Street, at the corner of Christopher and Bleeker Streets. Jon needed a roommate, and the apartment had a small bedroom behind the kitchen, so I could sleep on the couch in the small living room area. Believe me, it was an eye opener. There was no shower, but there was a bathtub in the kitchen under a counter that lifted up next to the sink. There was not only a regular lock, but also a bar that went diagonally from the floor to the door for additional security. Unlike at West Point, where we put our laundry in a bag once a week and left it in the hall to be picked up, I learned to walk a bag of laundry down six flights of stairs and two blocks down Bleeker to a laundromat. Jon was a musician, and we got along well. [35]

At first, it was exciting to be living in Greenwich Village. We were near Washington Square Park where steel drummers played constantly and I saw Dr. Hook and the Medicine Show introduce the Shel Silverstein song "Cover of the Rolling Stone." Jon played two recently released Grateful Dead albums for me, "American Beauty" and "Workingman's Dead," which I had not heard before. There was an ice cream shop we visited on Christopher Street a few doors from my apartment called Dave's Potbelly, where I first had Hagen Daaz ice cream in enormous sundaes. We could walk across the Village to the East Village and Tompkins Square Park, where Jon's friends lived. On the way, we passed the Fillmore East and the Electric Circus,

---

35 Jon not only was an excellent musician, he was very smart, as evidenced by his earning a degree from Goddard College in 1974 and later an MS from MIT in 1986 despite not finishing high school.

where you could walk in and see bands like Spirit, with its bald drummer. After three years at West Point, it was a welcome taste of freedom.

But as I started getting familiar with Greenwich Village, I received bad news: On September 3, 1970, Judge Marvin Frankel issued a long decision upholding the Army's denial of my application.[36] In his decision, Judge Frankel quoted at length from the Army Conscientious Objector Review Board's written final decision. I had not known that such a written decision existed, and I still have not received a copy from the Army, despite numerous FOIA requests.

This decision was significant because legally, Gleason's report was just a recommendation, and the Review Board decision I had never seen was what counted. Judge Frankel described the decision as follows:

> The Board held that petitioner's application must be denied. The exclusive ground of this determination was the conclusion that petitioner "lacks the depth of sincerity to qualify for discharge as a conscientious objector * * *." This finding, the opinion states, "is based on an objective analysis of facts found in the record." The Board found that petitioner's fundamental beliefs on the subject of central concern were not essentially different now from what they had been when he first entered the Academy. . . . The Board found that the initial failure of the petitioner to make his doubts "known to the proper officials" was at first "fully understandable," but that "his continued failure to express such growing feelings for over a period of two and one-half years makes his motives in not doing so suspect."

---

36 A copy of Judge Frankel's decision is included as Appendix 2.

—

As expressed in Parrott v. United States: "An average man of average intelligence who can read must daily realize that he may, once he is subject to a draft call from his local board * * * be soon called upon to kill." A U.S. Military Academy cadet who has spent over two years at the Academy certainly cannot be equated in knowledge of such matters with an average draftee, who conceivably might not know about the more necessary (albeit unpleasant and unfortunate) aspects of Army duty. Coming from a man with Donham's background, this statement is simply not believable.

Judge Frankel found that the board stressed that my concern about finishing the academic year was inconsistent with the required "depth of sincerity" needed to qualify for discharge under AR 635-20. What is most troubling about this summary by the Review Board is that it is not consistent with the reality of cadet life or of my interview with Gleason. I did share my feelings with a West Point chaplain, psychology professor and law professor. None recommended that I immediately go to my company tactical officer and discuss whether I should apply for discharge. And the Review Board failed to realize that cadets were not encouraged to share their feelings about the end result of military training—killing other humans. Rather, the emphasis was finishing the West Point ordeal and becoming an officer.

Judge Frankel's opinion also summarized my position, noting that the fact that I was candid in describing events that were not favorable could be viewed as evidence of my sincerity. He wrote that this, as well as the references who attested to my sincerity and integrity, "might prevail if this court were commissioned to decide independently his application for discharge from West Point as a conscientious objector." However, he continued:

> The court's role is a far more straitened one. As stated in petitioner's main brief, the judicial function here "is the limited one of determining whether there was a basis in fact for finding that he was not a conscientious objector * * *." More specifically, the question is whether the Conscientious Objector Review Board could rationally and honestly have concluded from the facts before it that petitioner had not demonstrated the requisite sincerity of his asserted convictions.

He concluded that the board had met this standard. To boil it down, Judge Frankel said that while if he were the first to rule on my application, he would likely grant it. However, under the law, he was only to consider whether the Army had a basis in fact to deny my application. He found that the Army did have a basis in fact to question my sincerity because it found that I had supposedly decided I was a conscientious objector in February but had held off submitting my application until after final exams. In other words, the Army could use the timing of my application as a factual reason to deny my discharge. The decision was especially disappointing to me because it was based on my answer to a question that had seemed innocent: "Why did you submit your application when you did?" "I wanted to finish my final exams." And somehow, Gleason decided that because the date when I first contacted a draft counselor was February, that was the date I had decided to apply as a conscientious objector, and that I had waited another three months before submitting my application just because I wanted to finish the semester. Gleason conveniently interpreted that as making me insincere. The judge felt constrained to accept Gleason's factual findings, which met the "basis in fact" necessary to sustain denying my application.

I still beat myself up for that answer because so much was behind it and I answered so quickly! I could have explained, I suppose, that I did not wake up one day and decide I was a conscientious objector. What was a conscientious objector? Was I really a conscientious objector? What went into an application and did it fit my actual frame of mind? When would I write it? Did I think an application would be successful and should that matter? Should I talk to a lawyer first? Where would I find and pay for a lawyer? How did one apply to be a conscientious objector in the Army? How would I describe my beliefs? What would my parents think? What would an application for discharge look like when it was done? How would I present it and when? How should I deal with classes while I was preparing my application? Even preparing the application once I decided to do so, as I have already explained, took weeks. I had to consider those questions, and I had no definite answers to them until I completed the application, collected the letters of recommendation, and was at a point where I felt I had to either submit it or give it up. But I also was proud of my grades and my academic standing, and I enjoyed my classes. Plus, after three years, I was so indoctrinated into the day-to-day West Point routine that breaking from it was really hard. Did that mean I was not sincere? Not in the least. The Army's approach, ironically, was not consistent with the "plan of attack" I had learned. Assuming I was the enemy, it seemed like it made no effort to learn who I was. Rather, its response was in the nature of "ready, fire, aim."

Once Judge Frankel ruled, I had to resign as a cadet. On September 10, 1970, I submitted the West Point-prepared resignation form. Surprisingly, given how anxious the academy had been to get rid of me since the end of May, the form wended its way through West Point and Army bureaucracy for another eleven days. It went from one staff officer at

West Point to another staff officer higher up the food chain and then up to the Superintendent, who recommended to the Army that my resignation be accepted, and finally the Army officially accepted my resignation on September 16—but I did not find out until September 21. Everything West Point had done since I submitted my application for discharge had been aimed at getting me out of the academy one way or another. While I knew this instinctively, I would not have believed the bureaucratic paper trail confirming this until I received West Point's response to my FOIA request many years later.

At this point, I was very discouraged. I was in a new form of limbo since I was now at the mercy of the Army, waiting for orders sending me to active duty. But the case wasn't over.

CHAPTER 16:

THINGS GO FROM BAD TO WORSE

Joan moved to reconsider Judge Frankel's decision. In the meantime, I still had to pay rent on the Greenwich Village apartment, one half of $95 dollars per month. (According to EasyStreet, average rent in that building a couple of years ago was about $3,700 per month, probably more now. I hope the apartments have been seriously updated.) I applied for jobs at several places, and by September 18, I was hired as a teacher's aide at IS 44, a middle school at 100 West 77th on Manhattan's Upper West Side, near the Natural History Museum. It was an interesting job, working with a racially and culturally diverse group of fifth-grade students. It turned out my knowledge of French was helpful because there were several students from Haiti, where French is one of the native languages. I wanted to make a difference, but the Army had other ideas. Shortly after I learned the Army had accepted my West Point resignation, I received an order requiring me to report to Ft. Campbell, KY on October 22. My work as a teacher's aide would be short-lived. I wrote West Point asking for a reprieve, even though I was not aware of any rule or practice that either allowed for or prohibited such a request:

> I.S. 44 ... contains approximately equal numbers of black, Spanish-speaking and white children. Many of the

children at the school are many years behind in their reading level and overall school performance.

I.S. 44 suffers from a shortage of the teachers it needs to cope with the problems of the children who are behind. As a matter of fact, the parents and teachers went out on strike at the beginning of the school year to have more teachers assigned to the schools. As a result, although I am not certified as a teacher, the major part of my job involves tutoring individuals in reading who are unable to stay with the normal classroom work. Because I am young and represent a "big brother" image to them, I relate very well to the children I help and I have been permanently assigned to a sixth grade class in which the average reading level is more than two years behind.

I therefore request that my call to active duty be delayed until the end of the school year, so as not further set back the children I teach.

West Point and the Army denied this request. A memo attached to the file copy of my letter had a single handwritten word: "Touching." Apparently, the Army's message to "be all that you can be" did not extend to working with poor minority children in New York City.

As hard as it was knowing I would have to leave my job, it was perhaps the easiest of the decisions I had to make in the month before I had to report to Ft. Campbell. One issue was whether I should report at all. If I refused to report, I would be AWOL—absent without leave. Being high profile, there was little doubt I would be arrested and prosecuted, and I would most likely be sentenced to a military prison for at least the rest of my three-year active duty term. I would also receive a dishonorable discharge from the Army and who knows what other punishments.

What worried Diane and me even more was that if I refused to report and ended up in Ft. Leavenworth or some other Army prison, would she even be able to visit me? We discussed whether we should go ahead and get married because we were sure that spouses could visit inmates. On the other hand, we had only been engaged for about three months and had known each other only about a year and a half. We had spent relatively little time together—weekends and a couple of weeks during my summer leave. We were certain we were in love, but how well did we really know each other? Neither of us had graduated from college, and our future was anything but certain. However, being young and naive, we ignored these obstacles and decided to go ahead and get married before I had to report for active duty. My parents were not happy, and I assume that Diane's parents had the same view. Still, at that point, I think they were just hoping for the best.

We arranged with Chaplain Easterling to perform the wedding. At this point, he knew Diane as well as me. We arranged for the ceremony to take place at his house on the West Point base on the evening of October 15, 1970. I was still twenty, and Diane had just turned twentyone a few days before. Diane and her friends picked out a long colorful dress for her to wear. I have no idea what I wore to the ceremony. We wrote part of our vows. Some of my former classmates and Diane's friends attended. We felt that we were doing what we had been planning to do anyway, just more quickly than we had planned to address an immediate issue.

I spoke several times with Joan about whether I should report. She encouraged me to report. She told me she wanted to reach out to my parents. I did not object, and she wrote them a long letter expressing her concern that I would not report, or that I would refuse an order if I reported to Ft. Campbell, and that she did not want me to do that. She told my parents that she believed I was very sincere and mentioned that there could be positions that would not require me to carry a weapon while my case was on appeal. She told me the same thing. My parents wrote her back expressing their appreciation for her support.

Later that month, the Army changed my reporting date to Monday, October 25. I bought tickets to fly to St. Louis on October 24, and I would take a bus about four hours to Hopkinsville, Kentucky, where Ft. Campbell was located. As a going-away present, Diane and I bought tickets to see Derek and the Dominos at the Fillmore East on Friday, October 23 (a concert that was later released as part of a live recording). The next day, I flew to St. Louis and was met by my parents. I bought my bus ticket and the next day was riding the Greyhound "dog" to Ft. Campbell. I had until midnight to report. It was a long, sad ride.

I reported to the unit where the Army had assigned me on a temporary basis. The unit commander, a young Captain, told me that he knew my background. He did not want any trouble during my temporary assignment in his unit as he was sure I soon would be reassigned to a more permanent assignment. He said he would not make me carry a weapon or take part in military exercise; he would assign me to work with the base chaplain. He encouraged me to accept this assignment, explaining that if I refused, he would have no choice but to lock me in the brig, and he did not want to do that—if for no other reason than that it would bring media attention. I wavered and asked if I could call my lawyer. I reached Joan, who spoke with the Captain, and he confirmed his offer. She advised me to accept the proposal. I would not be compromising my beliefs by working in the chaplain's office since I would not be carrying a rifle and not participating in military drills. I still wavered, but finally, she said that refusing an order would hurt my appeal. The appellate court would not look kindly, she said, if I defied a legitimate order. I accepted her advice. I was both disappointed and relieved. Part of me felt that refusing any order and being willing to suffer the consequences was the ultimate test of my sincerity, and I wondered if I failed that test. On the other hand, the appeal was the last hope for my application for discharge to be approved, and I did not really want to spend years in jail.

With those ground rules set, I became a soldier of sorts. I wore the green army uniform. The chaplain's office was in the Protestant chapel, a small white building with a steeple. The office itself was to the right as you entered the building through a small vestibule, and then the sanctuary with pews and a piano on the left side of the altar. My job was simply to show up and do whatever tasks the chaplain asked me to do. He was a kind man and assigned me mostly clerical tasks. I typed the Sunday bulletin, swept the chapel, ran errands, and helped take up the collection on Sundays. There were a lot of times that the chaplain was away, and I could read, write or play the piano. The Captain was true to his word: I did not ever have to carry a weapon or participate in military drills. I kept my head down and waited. And I speculated about what I would do if I were discharged. Should I move to Canada? Because "the way Nixon and Agnew have been talking really scares me, and most people seem to be right behind them, much more so in the Midwest and South than in the East. If I do stay in the US, it will probably be in New York. For some reason, I feel more comfortable there than in New Baden or St. Louis."

A week or two into my tenure as assistant, a young soldier came in to talk to the chaplain who was out, and we ended up talking. He was from the south, had been drafted and was very unsure about participating in a war. I mentioned that I was applying for discharge as a CO and explained a bit about the process. He seemed interested but, like many young draftees, seemed resigned to his fate. He had spent the past summer traveling with a gospel preacher and had played the organ at tent meetings. He showed me how hymns could be played gospel style. I watched him, and this chance

163

meeting really influenced my piano playing. I hope he was able to get out of the Army, but I suspect he did not as he did not have the support I did.

I stayed in a typical green Army barracks, two floors, rows of bunk beds facing each other across a middle aisle, and a latrine at the end of each floor. I got along well with most of the soldiers there, who were waiting for a new assignment. I found their attitudes to be similar to my West Point mailroom friends: the Army sucked, but whatever new assignment they received could only be worse. The main preoccupations at night were drinking cheap booze and writing letters. Occasionally, someone would read a book. I do not think there was a TV in the barracks.

I knew that Army bases often had "underground" newspapers, and I managed to find a soldier in my barracks who was involved in the one at Ft. Campbell, called *Napalm*. While I was there, I wrote a couple of articles that were published in that paper. The one I remember was called "ETS Early: CO Discharge," which explained how to apply for a conscientious objector discharge. (ETS stands for "expiration-term of service" and refers to the date a soldier will be discharged from the service. This was a very important date for most soldiers.)

On November 11, 1970, I turned twenty-one. There was no celebration. If I drank anything to celebrate, it was probably the cheapest cherry kijafa available, as that was the most popular beverage in the barracks. I wrote my parents on my birthday, "I'm reading a lot of books . . . . Last week, I read 'First Circle' by Solzhenitsyn and so far this week I've read 'Armies of the Night' by Mailer, a book of poems by Langston Hughes, a short book of Gandhi's philosophy, 'Amerika' by Kafka and 'Beneath the Wheel' by Herman Hesse."

I was not impressed with army life at Ft. Campbell. "No one in the army works—or at least few people do. Most jobs I've seen would make one person work about four hours a day if he worked fairly steadily, and those jobs usually have two or three men doing them."

Toward the end of November, I received new orders. My stint at Ft. Campbell ended around November 30, and I was to report to Ft. Sam Houston, Texas, by December 5 for medic training. The Army, despite claiming I wasn't a conscientious objector, ordered me to a position that conscientious objectors who were willing to serve in the military but who did not want to carry a weapon often held. It seemed like half a loaf, and not necessarily the good half.

My dad drove down to Ft. Campbell to pick me up; Diane flew to St. Louis and met me in New Baden. We only had a couple of days there because Joan wanted me to come to New York for the oral argument on my appeal before the Second Circuit Court of Appeals, scheduled for December 3. I caught a standby flight from St. Louis to New York City, and quickly sent a post card to my parents saying that I had no idea what would happen at the hearing the next day.

The Court of Appeals is located at 40 Centre Street in lower Manhattan, in an area known as Foley Square. The building, now known as the Thurgood Marshall United States Court House, is thirty-seven stories tall, with a six-story base and a thirty-story tower set back on the base. It is somberly guarded by twenty four-story columns that sit on an entry level reached by climbing a number of stairs. All in all, it was a very impressive and intimidating building.

I sat near the back of the imposing wood-paneled courtroom on the tower level. Three black-robed justices, all men, sat behind an elevated, highly polished bench. Since I was appealing, Joan went first, followed by the Assistant US Attorney. The justices interrupted the attorneys from time to time to ask questions that seemed, to my unpracticed ears, to be favorable to our position.

At the end of the argument, which took maybe fifteen to twenty minutes, we found out I was right in that impression. Joan told the justices that I was ordered to report again to active duty at Ft. Sam Houston in two days and asked the justices to stay that order. To my great surprise and elation, the court granted the stay from the bench while they considered the appeal. Once again, I was free, for the time being. Joan was happy, I was happy, Diane was happy and my parents were happy. We also were all relieved.

Diane was within weeks of graduating from Ladycliff a semester early, so I wanted to stay in New York. Luckily, Jon Gottlieb did not have another roommate yet, and he was glad to have me move back in. Also, despite his having left high school early, he had been admitted at Goddard College in Vermont. This was great for Jon, who was looking forward to leaving the city, and given his obvious talent and intelligence, Goddard College certainly deserved him. He was leaving by the end of the year.

That seemed to allow Diane the ability to move in once she graduated, but with rentcontrolled apartments, changing tenants was tricky. Someone had paid "key money" to someone, who had allowed Jon to take over the apartment. The actual "official" tenant was two or three steps down the line. I don't think Jon even knew who the real tenant was, and asking questions risked that person asking for more key money or, worse, finding a new tenant. The current lease extended through the following July, so we were safe until then.

Of course, I did not know how long the stay would keep me from active duty or what the appeals court decision would bring. In the meantime, I once again had to find a short-term job. It being Christmas season, I landed one in the toy department at Gimbel's Department Store near Herald Square and Pennsylvania Station, a block from Macy's. This was a perfect job because it was intended to be temporary, so I did not have to pretend I was looking for a permanent position. Back then, Gimbel's was a slightly lower-cost competitor of Macy's, and this was long before suburban box stores like Walmart and Best Buy or online retailers like Amazon proliferated. Department store shopping in Manhattan back then was still a big deal. Gimbel's was busy, especially the toy department. I knew nothing about toys or retail, but the store needed warm bodies, and I was one. I had to quickly learn what toys were popular, what toys were available, how to punch in and out, and especially how to work the large mechanical cash register while hand tracking inventory. It was a hectic job, but it was not the Army. I could hop on the A train to West 4th Street or the No. 1 IRT to Christopher Street and be home in less than half an hour. I could walk around Washington Square Park or stop in a club to see Rosalie Sorrels play, backed up by a young Dave Bromberg. I could see Diane on weekends. But there was still uncertainty. How would the Second Circuit rule, and when?

I left Gimbel's right around Christmas, when the temporary position ended. I do not recall what I did for the holiday. Maybe I stayed at 91 Christopher Street. Maybe I went to Rochester with Diane. Maybe I went home to New Baden. Whatever I did, I was in New York after Christmas, still waiting and jobless. Since I was once again in a bit of limbo, I found another temporary job down the street from Gimbel's at Macy's. I was hired to help take inventory and spent two or three weeks in the back rooms of Macy's, counting things like scissors and hairbrushes, eight hours a day. I did not really understand why I was counting scissors. After the blur of activity finding toys for customers and ringing them up at Gimbel's, the inventory job seemed like drudgery, but at least Diane had moved in to 91 Christopher Street and found a job with an actuarial firm in lower Manhattan, using her math major degree.

We were attending Washington Square Methodist Church on West 4th Street near Washington Square Park. The church was different from any I had attended before. Life on the street was interesting to say the least. One day, I stopped near the corner of West 4th Street and Avenue of the Americas and checked the pulse of a man lying on the sidewalk who appeared unconscious. A boy about twelve years old walked by and said, "You must be new here." There were restaurants offering different foods—I had never encountered cheese blintzes, for example.

Even though life was still uncertain, I was happy to be living with Diane, finally, and New York City was exciting and eye opening. I was hopeful.

CHAPTER 17:

MY APPEAL IS SUCCESSFUL

Everything changed again on January 6, 1971, this time for the better, when the Second Circuit reversed the district court's decision and sent my application for discharge back to the Army. The court summarized my application for discharge, explaining events that led to my application and noting that "[a] number of those with intimate contacts with Donham certified to the sincerity and depth of his evolving scruples of conscience."[37] It added that, as required by Army regulations, I was interviewed by a psychiatrist and chaplain, and each found I "was sincere in his convictions and a man of integrity." The Second Circuit noted Judge Frankel's comment that had he been the first to review my application, he might have granted it, but felt he was constrained to only determine if there was a basis in fact. The problem with Judge Frankel's ruling was that the bias and lack of knowledge of Col. Gleason tainted the entire process:

> [Donham] cites numerous instances of Colonel Gleason's total lack of knowledge concerning conscientious objection. He found that the applicant's religion must advocate conscientious objection, although this had apparently not been the law since the First World War. He was not aware

---

37 The full Second Circuit decision is included as Appendix 3.

of the elimination of religious requirements for conscientious objection. Moreover, Colonel Gleason apparently lacked the necessary objectivity to be a fair, knowledgeable hearing officer. He obviously and no doubt honestly could not believe that a West Point cadet could possibly develop conscientious scruples against war and assumed more the role of advocate than judge.

The Second Circuit found that Gleason's bias had materially affected the Army's decision: "If all three officers who had seen and heard petitioner (i.e., the psychiatrist and the chaplain who interviewed him and the hearing officer who observed him) had found petitioner sincere, the Army would have been hard pressed to justify its finding of insincerity." It remanded the case to the Army with instructions to assign a knowledgeable hearing officer, and it stayed orders sending me to active duty until the Army reheard my application.

The Army did not give up on the legal case after this decision, however. Later in January 1971, it filed a petition for rehearing with the Second Circuit, which the court denied on March 8. Almost immediately, on March 12, Assistant US Attorney Michael I. Saltzman wrote to Will R. Wilson, Assistant Attorney General in the Department of Justice Criminal Division in Washington, D.C., recommending against filing a petition for certiorari with the Supreme Court.[38] Rather, he recommended that the matter be remanded to the Army as the Second Circuit had ruled.

The Army was not pleased with Mr. Saltzman's recommendation. Upon receiving a copy of Mr. Saltzman's letter, the chief of litigation services for the Army's Judge Advocate General Corps, Colonel William B. Carne,

---

38 A petition for certiorari is the legal document a party files with the United States Supreme Court asking the Court to hear an appeal.

wrote directly to the United States Attorney General, John Mitchell.[39] The letter first complained that the Army "had not previously been advised of the Second Circuit's opinion." This seems unlikely, given the publicity my case received and the fact that the Assistant U.S. Attorney who represented the Army in the district court and Court of Appeals had to be communicating with the Army to obtain my records used in the case. Col. Carne went on to question how the Army should comply with the remand order. (That the Second Circuit's instructions to the Army to conduct a new hearing with a knowledgeable hearing officer were not clear to the Army is mind boggling.) The letter went on to say that despite the ruling that I was not to be ordered to active duty until the Army conducted a second, and this time fair, conscientious objector hearing, "we strongly believe that Donham has no right to remain away from active duty while his application is being reprocessed." Apparently, a Court of Appeals order was not good enough for the Army. Col. Carne continued, "We see no reason why Donham must be accorded any more than the Army regulation provides for those applying for conscientious objector discharge, i.e., assignment to duties providing minimal practicable conflict . . . . Accordingly, we request you advise us whether the stay is still in effect. If it is, we strenuously urge that Mr. Saltzman seek its dissolution." He closed by arguing that Mr. Saltzman was wrong to say that there was no substantial question of law for the Supreme Court to consider: "Accordingly, we believe that this case should be appealed to the Supreme Court." Colonel Carne's pleas, however, went for naught as my case was never appealed to the Supreme Court.

Thankfully, my inventory job at Macy's ended by mid-January. Even more thankfully, I was referred to the law firm of Fitelson & Mayer by the mother of one of Jon Gottlieb's friends, who was a secretary there. Fitelson

---

39 Mitchell resigned as Attorney General in 1972 to become the head of President Nixon's reelection campaign. He later served nineteen months in prison after being convicted of perjury, obstruction of justice and conspiracy in connection with the Watergate scandal.

& Mayer had been described a year earlier in a New York Magazine article as "the legal powerhouse of the theater world." Through Jon's contact, I was granted an interview with William Fitelson, the senior partner, who was politically liberal and an opponent of the Vietnam War. The file clerk for the firm was retiring, and he wanted to know if I would become the new file clerk. He had read about my case and was inclined to consider me favorably. I accepted.

My job was to try to organize the files that my predecessor had kept in such a way that she but no one else knew where to find anything. I suspect it was a form of job security. I also opened the plug-in switchboard in the morning and covered it when the regular operator was at lunch. When I arrived at the office, I was to bring a pitcher of water to Mr. Fitelson's office and open the windows about four inches. The firm was ahead of its time gender wise, as two of the seven partners were women, Floria Lasky and Adele Rubenstein.

The firm represented many of the established New York theater heavyweights: producer David Merrick, choreographer and director Jerome Robbins, playwright Edward Albee, author and director Elia Kazan, and actress Mary Martin. I did not meet all of these, but I certainly met and filed their legal documents and contracts. The firm also represented Shirley Booth in an unsuccessful attempt to hold Vita Herring liable for imitating her voice from the television show *Hazel*, and Gore Vidal in a libel suit with William F. Buckley. One morning, I answered a call to the office and a deep female voice asked, "Could I please speak to Mr. Fitelson?" As I was trained to do, I asked, "Can I tell him who's calling?" The response: "Katharine Hepburn."

Mr. Fitelson and the other partners liked me, and occasionally asked me to step out of my filing and "gopher" tasks. They had me do research on the Gore Vidal case. Partner Harold Sherman, who was representing

Gore Vidal in his lawsuit with William F. Buckley, sent me to the Lincoln Center for the Performing Arts Library and the New York Public Library to see if I could find evidence linking Buckley to 1930s anti-Semitic radio host Father Coughlin. Partner Benjamin Aslan sent me to the libraries to obtain background information about Shirley Booth to help respond to what I now know were discovery requests. And the firm let me take off a day in late April to attend the anti-war March on Washington, which drew nearly 500,000 protesters.

In June, Joan received word that the Army had scheduled my second conscientious objector hearing for June 16, 1971, at Ft. Hamilton, an Army base located on the waterfront in the southwestern corner of Brooklyn. All I knew about Ft. Hamilton was that it housed the chaplain school.

I again got the day off, and Joan and I trekked to Brooklyn for the hearing. The hearing officer was Major Donnell S. Mohr, who later retired as a Colonel in the US Army Reserve. Colonel Mohr had served in Vietnam and had earned a Bronze Star and the Air Medal. Many years later, he contacted me, and he told me that he had been selected as my hearing officer based on the Second Circuit's criticism of the West Point hearing officer's lack of knowledge of the law concerning conscientious objectors. Col. Mohr recalled in particular that Gleason had said that Methodists did not support conscientious objectors. Before the new hearing, Mohr spoke to a relative who was a military chaplain from the Methodist denomination. He learned that, certainly by the 1960 Methodist General Conference, the Methodist Church supported both those who were sincerely opposed to participating in war and those who believed they had a duty to serve the country in war.

The Army wanted a hearing officer who had heard more than one such case to avoid the same issue with the second hearing. By that time, then-Major Mohr had heard four conscientious objector cases, recommending granting CO status in two cases and denying it in two cases. One of his prior hearings involved a Jehovah's Witness, a faith whose members have long been recognized as conscientious objectors because their religion forbids them from swearing allegiance to anyone but God. The second successful applicant was a Jewish officer who had decided to become a missionary. The two whose applications Major Mohr had denied were, according to him, simply trying to get out of the Army.

June 16, 1971, was a clear day with a temperature around seventy degrees. I was not nearly as nervous as I had been a year earlier when I had faced Col. Gleason. The second hearing was very straightforward. The subtle and not-so-subtle animosity that had existed in all the prior West Point hearings was not present. There were no "gotcha" questions, I was better prepared and Major Mohr was familiar with cases such as *Welch v. United States*, a well-known draft case decided a year earlier, in January of 1970. In that case, the Supreme Court had made clear that religious beliefs were not required to obtain conscientious objector status. Supreme Court Justice Hugo Black had written that conscientious objector status applies to "all those whose consciences, spurred by deeply held moral, ethical, or religious beliefs, would give them no rest or peace if they allowed themselves to become a part of an instrument of war." Joan and I thought the hearing had gone well, and I felt optimistic.

We were correct in our assessment. Major Mohr told me that his mission was just to follow the law; I now know that he wrote a report recommending that my application be granted and that I be discharged as a conscientious objector. To date, the Army has not provided this report to me in any FOIA response. However, I learned from Major Mohr that behind the scenes, the Army was trying to coerce him to change his report. Shortly after he issued it, he found his mail being steamed open. He received a telephone call one evening from an anonymous person trying to disguise his voice. This person said he was a senior officer in the Army and an ACLU "mole." He said that the Nixon administration was out to get Major Mohr and that he must be "as pure as Caesar's wife." Major Mohr later received a telephone call from a Colonel in the Army Department of Personnel. He said he had been asked by an officer in the White House (who had to be Wilfred Ebel, a political appointee who served in several Republican administrations) that the "highest office in the land"—i.e. the president— was disturbed by Major Mohr's decision to recommend approval of my application. The Colonel went so far as to order Major Mohr to change his decision. Major Mohr responded, "You have ordered me to obey an unlaw- ful order," and refused. His superiors continued harassing him and placed a letter in his personnel file stating that he was unfit for further command and military education, which was a prerequisite for his potential promo- tion to Lieutenant Colonel. Major Mohr, tired of the bullying, resigned his regular commission at the end of 1971 and joined the Army Reserves.

At the time, we had no idea this internal Army maneuvering was occurring. Once again, we were just waiting. That summer after my second hearing, I felt a weight begin to lift. I was working at a job I liked and Diane had a job with an actuarial firm where she could use her math degree. We could sample inexpensive restaurants in the Village, and go to shows at the Fillmore East, where we saw the Band, Van Morrison, Quicksilver Messenger Service, the drummer Buddy Rich and Ravi Shankar. We saw Joan Baez and the Byrds at Carnegie Hall. We became friends with Izzy Young, who ran the Folklore Center on 6th Avenue near West Fourth Street.

During the 1960s, he had encouraged many folk artists including a young Bob Dylan.

My brother Mark visited us for a week or so. He had come from Chicago by way of Virginia Beach where he and friend had formed a duo that had played regularly in a club called Ratso's in Chicago. He mentioned a man he had met in his travels who called himself Gypsy Jim, who claimed to be a traveling musician. One day we were walking down West Fourth Street toward 6th Avenue when Mark, who had been in New York City about twenty-four hours, yelled out "Jim, what are you doing here?" It was Gypsy Jim, playing his guitar on a street corner, looking for tips. I ran into Jim several times over the next few months, and I even wrote a song about him.

At the same time, Diane and I were deciding what to do when our time at 91 Christopher Street ran out at the end of July. Mr. Fitelson had made me an offer that was difficult to refuse: he said he would continue to employ me while I finished college and then would pay for me to go to law school. It was an unbelievable opportunity. How do you refuse such an offer, especially when the firm was central to the New York theater world? But I did.

While living on Christopher Street, we had started attending the Washington Square Methodist Church, on West Fourth Street between Sixth Avenue (Avenue of the Americas) and McDougal Street on the West edge of Washington Square Park. The sign on the church's message board called it the "Peace Church." We learned from the pastor, Rev. George Hill, that a few years earlier, the 1966 Christmas Eve service at the church had been televised. The pastor at that time, Rev. Finley Schaef, had the pews unbolted so they could be moved around and the service was unconventional. In the years after, the church became known as the Peace Church. It hosted a day care center, a draft counseling center and a meeting place for the Vietnam Veterans Against the War. The congregation included a wide variety of people—artists, activists, writers, and members of the LGBTQ community. We were welcomed by the small congregation.

The church, in addition to the pastor, employed a janitor, Robert Earl Jones—the father of actor James Earl Jones. It also had received funding for a youth director position, and the prior youth director was leaving. I applied for the position, and the members approved of me being hired, to start August 1, 1971. I reluctantly turned down Mr. Fitelson's offer. Part of my reasoning was that as a conscientious objector, I should be doing God's work. The law firm was fascinating, but I felt like I would be taking advantage of my conscientious objector application if I turned down the youth director position.

The position had two related functions. The Methodist Center for the United Nations would host groups of teenagers from all over the country for several days, and they would bring the groups to Greenwich Village for an evening. We would walk the groups around Greenwich Village and Washington Square Park and then have group discussions about subjects that the out-of-towners would likely not have heard about. I would discuss my West Point case and the Vietnam War. A friend discussed being gay and gay liberation.[40] Young women would discuss women's liberation. The groups would ask questions and, when the evening program ended, would often leave with eyes glazed. In addition, on occasion, the church would host New York area youth groups for weekend sleepovers. The position did not pay much—$250 per month— but it came with a rent-free apartment with four large rooms on the fourth floor of the manse, located next to the church.

About two weeks after I started my job at the church, I received a telegram telling me to report to Fort Dix, New Jersey, to be discharged. I am not sure if I had ever received a telegram before. I was standing in our bedroom at the church house at 125 W. Fourth Street, which was on the fourth floor. Diane and I were excited, but a bit unclear. The telegram said

---

40 "Gay liberation" was the term used in our discussions back then.

I should report to Ft. Dix to be discharged, but it didn't say anything more. Of course, I called people—my parents, Joan, even Chaplain Easterling at West Point. On one hand, I was not going back in the Army. But would I have to do alternate service? Would I have to leave my job at the church? Or would I be free to go back to college and finish my undergrad degree?

But first I had to get to Ft. Dix. Since Diane and I did not have a car, I had to go by bus. Although Ft. Dix is only about eighty miles from New York City, the bus ride took nearly two and a half hours. I was expecting a typical army hassle, but the processing went smoothly. I even saw a former West Point cadet classmate who had left the academy and was now an enlisted man working in the administration office. He congratulated me.

To my surprise, I was not granted CO status. Instead, I was honorably discharged with no reserve duty and no alternative service. It was as if the Army wanted to totally wash its hands of me. I had an honorable discharge certificate signed by General Westmoreland. I had challenged the Army and prevailed—although I would have preferred to have been granted CO status, which would have confirmed that I was and had always been sincere in my beliefs. On the other hand, and importantly, I had an official DD214 form confirming I had served and had no further military obligations. It wasn't until much later that I learned, as I discussed above, that my second hearing officer had recommended that I be granted a CO discharge. I concluded that granting me a CO discharge would have required the Army to admit it had been wrong and would have been too much crow for it to swallow. Still, I was ecstatic—but even more, I was relieved. Whatever my future held, it would not involve choosing whether or not to kill people in a meaningless and immoral war. [41]

---

41 There were brief press reports about my being discharged. The most memorable to me was a *New York Daily News* editorial, "Conchy Goes Scot Free."

I have much more recently obtained, through FOIA, a "Fact Sheet" dated September 30, 1971, that was prepared by Staff Judge Advocate Colonel Oldham. The purpose of the "Fact Sheet" was to inform the West Point Superintendent of final action in my case. The Fact Sheet reads that "on 15 April 1971, Department of the Army reprocessed Donham's conscientious objection application, approved it and discharged him from the service in August 1971." As was often the case with Army records, it raises as many questions as it answers. For example, if the Army had re-processed and approved my application in April 1971, why did it go through the charade of a re-hearing in June of that year? Or was Col. Oldham just mistaken about the dates?

Despite repeated attempts, the Army has refused to provide any further information about its apparent approval of my CO request and its later decision to simply award me an Honorable Discharge.

CHAPTER 18

LIFE GETS IN THE WAY

We celebrated over the next few days as I started my new job and was accepted at Hunter College to finish my degree. Things looked bright. But that soon changed as life caught up with me.

Diane and I were not prepared for the fast-paced, radical environment the church fostered. We had gotten married when we did because we were concerned that I might be arrested and jailed for disobeying an order. But when I was granted a discharge, and not a conscientious objector discharge, I believe Diane was in a way disappointed. I had followed my lawyer's recommendation to accept the chaplain's assistant position to avoid being jailed. Did she see that as too much of a compromise? Maybe I was not the war resister people like David Harris—Joan Baez's then-husband, who served time in federal prison from July 1969 to March 1971 for resisting the draft—were. Maybe we were just too young. Whatever the reason, by November 1971, I learned she had been unfaithful. We separated less than a year after I received my discharge.

I began my first semester at Hunter College enthusiastically, but as my marriage continued to unravel, I became depressed and less diligent. One of my professors first semester at Hunter had nominated me for a Danforth Fellowship, and I had to take the GRE. By the morning of the exam, I was so distraught I had stayed up most of the night before high on drugs, probably LSD. My scores were okay but not great. I managed to finish the first semester with As in four of five subjects, but in the subject where I should have excelled, political science, I received an incomplete. It was startling how quickly my excitement at being discharged had changed to anger and frustration. Today, someone might have suggested that I get help. At the time, I was so embarrassed and felt like such a failure that I could not even talk to the pastor of the church about how I felt, so I just tried to keep going. I would take a train to 42nd Street, take the shuttle to Grand Central Station and then get on the IRT uptown toward Hunter College. I would go to the door of the class, almost inevitably a few minutes late. Rather than go to the class, I would turn around and retrace my steps to Greenwich Village. In the spring of 1972, I went for an interview with members of the selection committee for the fellowship, but I did not take it seriously. I was underdressed and angry. Unsurprisingly, I did not get it.

I did help organize the New York Switchboard, which gathered information on free services for young people looking for alternatives to more traditional travel services. We also tried to help runaways. I worked occasionally with some friends from the switchboard who did low-cost moving, using a van someone owned. We went by the name Commune Movers.

Around Memorial Day, I went with three friends to Europe, getting a cheap flight on Icelandic Airlines to Luxembourg. The round-trip flight cost about $160. Before I left, I sent a letter to my parents telling them that Diane and I were done.

We all went to Paris first, and then I was on my own, with plans to meet back in Luxembourg for our flight home. I hitchhiked, carrying a backpack and a cheap guitar, from Paris to Amsterdam, where I stayed for a few days in a youth hostel and one night sleeping in the Vondelpark.

Next, to Oostende, Belgium, for a ferry boat to England. After that, to London, where I stayed with three women I had met in Amsterdam who had invited me to their flat. Then, I hitchhiked to Edinburgh, Scotland, where I arrived on June 21—midsummer night—and the sun was out until midnight. From Edinburgh, I decided to go to Belfast, Ireland, by ferry from Stranraer on the west coast of Scotland. 1972 was the time of the troubles in Northern Ireland, and I was decrepit-looking after four weeks of hitchhiking. I was still carrying a guitar and a backpack and was sporting long hair, a scruffy beard, and a worn fedora. During my travels, I had picked up flyers from radical groups in Europe such as the now infamous Red Army Faction from Germany. During the trip across the Irish channel, Irish police questioned me about where I was going and why. I guess I answered acceptably, as they left me alone, but I did not want to hitchhike in Northern Ireland. Fortunately, I met a young Scottish journalist who offered to drive me from the ferry to Dublin, but we agreed to drive through Belfast first. The tension was thick. British troops patrolled the streets in jeeps, with young, terrified soldiers holding automatic rifles riding in the back. We decided to leave quickly. As we drove south across the border to the Irish Republic, a guardhouse by the border was burning. After a night in Dublin, I hitchhiked to Cork, on the south west corner of Ireland where I stayed in a hostel for a few days.

I ended up returning to Luxembourg by bus, ferry and train in time to meet my friends and return to New York City. The anti-Nixon campaign was in full swing, and Diane had moved to Washington, D.C., to work on it. I was growing increasingly angrier and questioning my faith. After Nixon was reelected in a landslide, I decided to quit my job at the church and, with few options and less money, moved to Macomb, Illinois, where my brother Mark had started college.

My experiences had made me very suspicious of large institutions. I did not trust the Army, the government, large corporations, New York City or even organized religion. When I left New York and moved to the run-down farmhouse near Macomb, Illinois, that Mark rented in November 1972, I was angry and contemptuous of people who were inclined to accept the status quo.

My cynicism only increased when I was diagnosed with insulin-dependent (Type 1) diabetes in May 1973. I had to learn about diet and taking insulin shots and being aware of low blood sugar reactions. The thought crossed my mind briefly that if I had stayed in the Army, I would have received a medical discharge. Then I learned that the doctor I had been assigned to at the McDonough County Hospital, Dr. Berrios, had been fired, but the hospital wouldn't say why.

I now know he was incompetent and the advice he gave me was dangerous.

Even when I was accepted later that year at Western Illinois University in Macomb on a scholarship to finish my undergraduate degree, I looked down on the college. I thought the students living in dorms were hopelessly naïve. I thought most of the professors I had were losers, who were teaching at Western Illinois because it was the only college that would hire them. There were two exceptions: Dr. Loren Logsden, an American literature professor who taught a course in science fiction literature and in a 1973 class had the class read "First Blood" by James Morrell, which introduced the Rambo character nine years before the first movie was released; and Dr. Karen Rosenblum Cale, a chain-smoking political science professor from New York City who attracted a group of left-leaning students to her classes and to gatherings in her apartment. I graduated in 1974 but I did not bother to attend my graduation.

My cynical view at that time was that institutions were to be taken advantage of to the extent possible, so I applied as a graduate student to the Western Illinois Political Science Department and was accepted. Then, I applied to become a paid graduate assistant and was accepted. But when the university fired Professor Dr. Rosenblum Cale, who was the chair of my master's thesis committee, my contempt for education was complete and I dropped out to take a job with the Western Illinois Regional council, a five-county planning commission. Even with this job, I felt I was working the "system" because it was funded by the federally funded CETA program. [42]

When I was in Macomb, I rekindled my interest in music, which had dwindled since West Point. I studied blues and old folk records. I began again to write songs, and Mark and I formed bands that played in the Western Illinois area. In 1977, after a year in the CETA job, I decided to leave Macomb, and moved to Chicago with the goal of, for the first time in my life, making a living playing music.

What is amazing is that it worked out as if it were planned. I traveled to Chicago to stay with some friends (Mary Ann Ryan, Patrice Ceisel, and Barbara Malone) for a couple days, while I was looking for an apartment. On the first day, I found an inexpensive studio apartment two blocks from Wrigley Field. On the second day, my friends took me to a couple bars where they thought I would like the music. The first was Mr. Kiley's, which had a house band called Free Wheel; it played country rock five nights a week with a popular willowy blond female singer. I learned the band was looking for a piano player. A couple weeks later, I returned and auditioned and got the job.

Let me digress for a minute about Mr. Kiley's. The great thing about playing in a house band was steady work, not having to move or

---

42 CETA was an acronym for the Comprehensive Employment and Training Act, federal jobs program operated through the Department of Housing and Urban Development.

set up equipment and being paid in cash. Free Wheel played country rock Tuesdays through Fridays from 9pm to 4am and on Saturdays from 9pm to 5am. I saw playing music night after night to be a way of bringing people together for a positive experience. Not to compare myself to Bruce Springsteen, but he had made a similar comment:

> I was looking for some way to put my music to some service on a nightly basis. You go into a town, you play a little music, you leave something behind. That idea connected us to the local community. It was a very simple idea, but it really resonated with me. —
>
> Springsteen, "Born to Run" (2016).

So being a musician was, to me, consistent with being an opponent of war and violence, even in an urban honkytonk like Mr. Kiley's.

Free Wheel's guitar and fiddle player, tall with reddish curly hair, said he loved Mr. Kiley's because you felt you were doing something illegal when you stepped inside the bar. Pinball machines, dancers, Old Style beer and good music: what you saw was what you got. One of my favorite memories of Mr. Kiley's was when I was approaching the bar one summer evening and all of a sudden a barstool came flying out the front door. A minute later, a guy came flying out, followed by doorman Pete grinning and rubbing his hands together. Pete was a fixture in the three summers I was at Mr. Kiley's. He must have been around his late fifties, with snow white hair and a scary smile. He was generally polite to guests, but God help anyone who made trouble.

Frank Kiley, Jr. was the bar manager. Frank was a very big man, very tough but basically fair, for a rough-and-tumble Chicago late-night bar owner. Our fiddle player, J.B., referred to him privately as the human slug, based on his physical appearance. Since Free Wheel was popular—the joint was jammed on Fridays and Saturdays and often during the week—Frank did not care what we played, so among the Merle Haggard, Emmylou Harris, Linda Ronstadt and Waylon Jennings songs we did a number of original songs that members of the band wrote. The bar was popular enough that on occasion, musicians passing through Chicago jammed with the band. Gregg Allman and Dicky Betts of the Allman Brothers Band, Elvin Bishop, Steve Goodman and John Prine were among those who jammed with Free Wheel.[43] Once, Robin Williams walked into Mr. Kiley's, to much excitement. I, however, never even saw him, as I was working on a high scoring game on a pinball machine, and couldn't be bothered.

Frank was also very practical. Take the beer menu. When I joined Free Wheel, you had your choice of Old Style beer, bottle or draft. Later, he brought in Old Style Lite and Heineken's. (At least that is what the bottles said.) Very easy for the bartender and the consumer. And Frank could be quick on his feet. One fall Saturday night, when daylight saving time ended, at midnight, the clock "fell back" an hour. That meant that we played the equivalent of 9pm–6am, an hour longer than usual. I said to Frank that we should get some extra pay since we played an extra hour. Frank responded, "I don't remember you giving me money back in the spring when the clock moved forward and you played an hour less." Implacable logic!

One night, my electric piano malfunctioned, and I was looking at it during a break. A pretty blond woman came up to the stage with a couple of her friends and asked if I needed help fixing the piano, explaining that she was adept at mechanical things. One of her friends assured me, "She can fix anything!" She also said her friends had bet her that she wouldn't ask me if I needed help, and if she did, they would buy her a beer. I asked

---

43 An aspiring rock and blues photographer, Kirk West, who had photographed the Allman Brothers show and who sometimes stopped in Mr. Kiley's, brought them to the bar. Kirk went on to travel with the Allman Brothers for twenty years and is considered one of the great blues and rock and roll photographers. He also photographed Becky's and my wedding.

her name, and she said Becky. I thanked her and declined. During the next weeks, I then noticed that she was a regular in the bar, listening, dancing and drinking a coke. We started talking during breaks and I learned she was working as a lighting designer and technician in Chicago theaters. She lived in a coach house less than a block from the bar and had lived for a year and a half in New York City. We both agreed that we hated that city (we did agree, however, that we liked a downstairs Chinatown restaurant at 17 Mott Street called Wo Hop, which is still open). One day, a few days before Memorial Day of 1978, I was returning from a run along the lakefront and we ran into each other on the sidewalk near the corner of Belmont and Sheridan Avenues. She looked at me and said, "Don't I know you?" and I answered, "I guess so." We walked back together to her coach house apartment a few doors from Mr. Kileys's, and a few days later, she asked me if I wanted to come to a play, "Prague Spring," where she was running the lights that Sunday. She even said she had two tickets if I wanted to bring someone along. I didn't. That Sunday was our first date.

By fall, we were beginning to see a future together. In February 1979, we moved in together, while Chicago streets were lined with four foot tall snow drifts. While we were living together, two incidents made us decide to get married. First, I was accosted coming back from Mr. Kiley's on Halloween night by two men, one who had a Saturday night special gun. I had only a couple dollars in my wallet, but I was carrying a bag with harmonicas I played. I gave the robbers what money I had, showed them the harmonicas and asked if they wanted the harmonicas too. They said no. Then one said, "Is that really all you got?" When I said it was, and that I was just a musician coming home from a gig, they looked at each other, and then one asked "You need carfare?" I declined this offer and they left me alone. Then, one morning, I had a severe insulin reaction at a grocery store and passed out. Paramedics were taking me to an emergency room and the store manager called our apartment. Becky ran and joined the ambulance, and convinced the nurses at the hospital I was a diabetic and was not over-dosing on drugs. Those intense events led us to decide that we needed to be married. So after living together for a year and a half, we were married on June 22, 1980. We have now been married forty-two years.

My relationship with Becky was the beginning of crawling out of eight years of cynicism, although it was not always a straight path. While I made a living playing in different bands for the next five years, I witnessed how drug and alcohol can weigh down talent and kill ambition. We some-times struggled financially, and I went through another bout of depression when music opportunities dried up for me in 1983 and 1984.

One day in 1984, it struck me, out of the blue, that I was only thir-ty-four years old, and maybe I could move myself in a different direction. I had been fascinated by the law since I had devoured Perry Mason books as a kid. My interest had continued while I was at West Point and it was central to my CO application. I had signed up to take the Law School Admissions Test (LSAT) while I was in Macomb but had blown the test off to play a music gig. And I had a good friend, Ivan Strunin, who was going to law school at night. He and I had played in bands together and he had a job that reimbursed his tuition. I decided to look into law school—again—and found out that I could take the LSAT the very next Saturday. If I did well, I could possibly be admitted in time for the fall 1984 semester. I did well enough not only to be admitted to night school at Chicago Kent School of Law, but also to get a scholarship. Ivan helped me get a job at Commerce Clearinghouse (CCH), a law publishing company, where he worked. Like him, I went to night school while I worked at CCH days, and between the scholarship and a tuition reimbursement program at my job, I ended law school nearly debt-free. Admittedly, working full time and going to night school four years straight was a challenge for Becky and our marriage, but we made it work.

As I did well in law school and at CCH, I believe going into law was what we Presbyterians refer to as a calling. For no obvious reasons, things just fell into place, which now leads me to believe God was playing a role. My grades were high enough to earn a spot as a law review editor and, after graduation, to obtain a clerkship with a federal magistrate judge, Elaine E. Bucklo. I worked two years as Judge Bucklo's law clerk, and then was offered a position with a Chicago law firm, Shefsky & Froelich, where I worked for thirty years. Practicing law has been a constant balance between what is right and wrong and what is convenient and what is ethical.

To me, it is a search for justice.[44]

One cannot succeed working days and going to school if one is cynical. Gradually, my cynicism continued to wane, and it disappeared when our son Sam was born in 1993. You cannot be cynical when raising a child. Parenthood brought Becky and me to our roots: how do you instill moral values when you raise a son? In 1994, we began attending Fourth Presbyterian Church on Michigan Avenue in downtown Chicago. Becky had gone there with her father as a teenager after her parents' divorce and thought it would be a good place to start as we looked for a church. We were enthralled by Rev. John Buchanan's sermons, and we met other families with young children. We became members, and became active, Becky as a Sunday school teacher and me as a member of the Children and Family Committee. I was ordained as a Deacon, and both Becky and I have become Stephen Ministers there. My faith was back.

---

44 Ironically, in 2014 Shefsky & Froelich merged with another Midwest law firm, Taft Stettinius & Hollister, the "Taft" being the late conservative Republican senator from Ohio, Robert Taft. In 2020, I retired as a Taft partner.

And as my faith returned, so did my conscious opposition to war. I thought the invasion of Grenada was absurd, just an ego boost for then President Reagan. However, it did not stir outrage like Vietnam did. I had been uncomfortable with the first Iraq War, Desert Storm, the five-week battle in January and February 1991. Going to war over Iraq's land grab, at a cost of nearly 5,000 civilian lives and the destruction of Iraq's and Kuwait's infrastructure, seemed out of proportion. Fortunately, that war was short-lived. But the second Iraq War, based on the phony premise that Iraq had weapons of mass destruction, demonstrates very clearly that the men who decide that our country (or any country for that matter) should go to war do so as grand masters, using young idealistic men and women as their pawns—in other words, "Let's you and them fight."

Of course, after the September 11, 2001, attacks, I felt that the world had changed for the worse. I told our eight-year-old son that day that things would never be the same. Our family was at Presbyterian weekend camp in October 2001. As the campers were departing on a soggy Sunday afternoon, the camp director announced that he had heard that the United States had started bombing Afghanistan. My heart sank because this seemed like we were stepping in quicksand, much like we did in Vietnam—once we started there, we would be stuck and never get out. My premonition was accurate because twenty years later, we have only recently departed Afghanistan with little to show for the money and lives expended over that time. And we are left again with the vexing question of how to resolve conflict in a way that does not destroy lives, property, jobs and economies. I will say it again: war is not the answer.

CONCLUSION

My confrontation with the Army has had a profound impact on my life. It has made me wary of those who exercise power arbitrarily, without a sense of morality or even logic.

Thankfully, I am not alone in this concern.

In 1963, Dr. Martin Luther King, Jr. wrote, in his Letter from a Birmingham Jail, "Injustice anywhere is a threat to justice everywhere. We are caught in an inescapable network of mutuality, tied in a single garment of destiny. Whatever affects one directly affects all indirectly." I had not read that famous letter while I was preparing my application for discharge, but it says succinctly what I was trying to say then and believe now. We are all connected, and war destroys that connectedness. In particular, civilian casualties are relegated to "collateral damage," whether it was the oxymoron from Vietnam that "we had to destroy that village in order to save it" or the August 29, 2021 drone strike at the Kabul, Afghanistan, airport gate that killed ten innocent civilians rather than the intended terrorists.

But mistakes and "collateral damage" are inevitable on the battlefield, and isn't war an unfortunate but sometimes necessary step toward achieving peace? Not really. Let's consider what peace means. Many people, ranging from Einstein and Spinoza to Pope John Paul II and President Obama, have said that peace is not just the absence of war, as devastating as the "realistic" and "practical" effects of war are. Rather, peace is the presence of justice, a spirit of cooperation and confidence in the future, the ability to resolve conflict by peaceful means. The longing for a just peace is a component of faith. Through my struggle with the Army, I came face to face with the need to have faith to carry on, and while my faith has at times waned, it has served me throughout my life. To me, faith in its best sense is acting on Jesus' teachings even though there is no guarantee that he was the son of God. As the man with the epileptic child who came to Jesus seeking help said, "Lord, I believe; help my unbelief." My faith still compels me to reject war as a solution to disagreements, even those that may seem intractable and even though wars seem inevitable given human history. So, if I were in the same situation again, knowing what I now know, would I apply for discharge as a conscientious objector again? The answer is yes.

Back in 1967, I believed I had a duty to serve, and I did my best to make it a reality by attending the United States Military Academy at West Point. However, after three years of military indoctrination, I came to a radically different conclusion and realized that my moral and religious beliefs did not allow me to be part of the war machine.

The Army and West Point treated me as a threat and a pariah, tried to discredit me and ultimately concealed that an officer had recommended that my application for a conscientious objector discharge be granted. In fact, a document I received from my FOIA requests suggests that my application was at least initially granted. Sadly, not much has changed in the past fifty years. Those in the military who publicly express deeply held moral and ethical beliefs that oppose the status quo are ignored or face unfortunate and disparaging treatment. In 2004, Captain Peter Brown, a West Point graduate, applied for discharge from the Army as a CO. While just as in my case his chaplain and psychiatrist recommended discharge, the Army refused. Only after Capt. Brown filed a lawsuit challenging the Army's decision did it relent and grant his request. A wholly different and extremely tragic recent example is the murder of Spc. Vanessa Guillen at

Ft. Hood, Texas, who faced regular sexual harassment within her unit. Spc. Guillen told a supervisor and some of her peers, who also passed this information on to her supervisor, who did nothing. Finally, a fellow enlisted soldier killed and dismembered Spc. Guillen. While the Army recently disciplined those in her chain of command, this is small comfort to her family. The Army's reluctance to listen to those who speak truth to power also extends to Navy Captain Brett Crozier, commander of the *U.S.S. Roosevelt*. Capt. Crozier was relieved of his command by the civilian Secretary of the Navy after he wrote an urgent letter seeking more help for his crew in dealing with the COVID-19 outbreak, after the letter became public. And as I mentioned above, sixteen African–American female graduating cadets were singled out for counseling by the Commandant of Cadets just because they enthusiastically raised their fists in celebration in pre-graduation photos. Will the military ever learn that it should not treat internal critics as the enemy?

But our country survived the Vietnam War, and I remain hopeful that it will survive the multiple crises we are facing in 2022 and will continue to face in the near future. While my view that war is unacceptable was not and likely is not popular, it is a view that deserves to be heard because ignoring the morality of war weakens the country's moral fiber. Simply accepting war as inevitable also impedes what Martin Luther King Jr. referred to as the arc of the universe bending toward justice. Facing the immediate consequences of taking a moral stand against authority was life-changing for me, but it was not life-ending. I struggled, and even lost my faith for a time, but regained it stronger than ever. Whatever else you do, whatever mistakes you may make, you will always know that when you faced a choice between the easier wrong and the harder right, you chose the harder path, and when you look in the mirror, you can look yourself in the eye.

ACKNOWLEDGEMENTS

This memoir was made possible by the love, assistance, encouragement and editing of my wife, who not only reminded me I should tell my story, but read and re-read the manuscript to make it better. Also, my son Sam Donham pushed me to finish the book. I need to offer special thanks to my former law partner Lloyd Shefsky, who read and helped me with the manuscript and told me my book needed to be published. My editor, Madeleine Vasaly, provided invaluable insights and assistance as did the cover designer, Susan Fitzpatrick Cornelison. Rev. Lucy Forster-Smith, Senior Associate Pastor at Fourth Presbyterian Church in Chicago, read an early draft and gave me advice and encouraged me to continue working on it. I also appreciate the encouragement from my long-time friend Ivan Strunin, who kept reminding me that I should tell my story, and my wife's friend, former librarian, Debbie McLeod, who also took the time read and comment on an early version of the manuscript. My West Point roommate Les LeMieux read drafts and supported my writing efforts. Livia Binks offered support and advice for this entire project. In addition, my former legal assistant Paula Bishton helped with word processing over the years when as I worked on my story, as did a "floater" secretary at the law firm, Alma McDonald, a Marine veteran who after reading the first three chapters said I should finish the book; and Charlie Riley, who helped organize the Army's FOIA response for me. I appreciate Col. Donnell Mohr, who told me about how the government interfered with his recommendation that I be discharged as a CO and who paid a professional price for his recommendation. I should also mention Stephen Minister friends from Fourth Presbyterian Church, who said I should write this memoir. And I want to thank my former law partner and friend John F. Kennedy, not because of what he did but because of who he is (and because I promised him I would mention him).

Finally, thanks to my lawyer, Joan Goldberg, to Rev. Michael Easterling, and to my late parents, Sam and Laura Donham, who stood with me when I left West Point and saved the letters I sent home, without which this memoir would not have been possible.

ABOUT THE AUTHOR

Born in 1949, Cary Donham grew up in small towns in downstate Illinois. After moving to the small town of New Baden, Illinois, he excelled in academics and athletics, and in 1967 received an appointment to the United States Military Academy at West Point. There, after three years and despite being in the top ten percent of his class academically, his religious upbringing and beliefs led him to apply for discharge from the Army as a conscientious objector.

After prevailing in a federal court lawsuit, and receiving an honorable discharge from the Army, he worked in a Greenwich Village Church, then moved back to Illinois where he finished his undergraduate degree from Western Illinois University. In 1978, he moved to Chicago where he made a living for five years as a musician and as an over-the-transom writer for the Chicago Reader. He applied to law school in 1984, was accepted, and attended law school at night while working full time, finishing fifth in his class, and being published in the Chicago Kent Law Review.

After graduating from law school in 1988, he clerked in federal court for two years, then worked at a Chicago law firm for 30 years, becoming a partner in 1996. He and his wife of 42 years now reside in Kentucky.

APPLICATION FOR DISCHARGE

RELIGIOUS TRAINING AND BELIEF

a) A description of the nature-of-belief which is the basis; of claim:

My beliefs concerning war stem from a belief in God and in the New Testament teachings of Christ. For me, the heart of Christianity is love: Jesus said, "Thou shalt love the Lord thy God with thy whole heart, and with thy whole soul, and with thy whole strength and with thy whole mind, and thy neighbor as thy-self.: (Luke 10, 27) He also taught his disciples to return love for hatred, to turn the other cheek, to love not only one's friends but also one's enemies. In a letter to the Corinthians, the apostle Paul states, "Faith, hope, and love, these three; but the greatest of these is love." (1 Cor 13, 13) According to Soren Kierkegaard, the New Testament makes loving a commandment, a demand made on all Christians.

—

---

45 Additional documents referenced in this book can be found at my website, https://peaceandpolitics.com/.

Each person, each individual is a necessary part of the world, and no person is expendable.

My place in this world is not to pass judgment on these other individuals. The New Testament teaches that we should love everyone, not only those who agree with our thoughts or support our government. Thus, I have no right to take the life of any other person since he is a necessary and special part of the universe, someone whom I have a duty to love. Ira Sandperl said, "the only truth, for me, is that no one knows the truth, and therefore no one has the right to take another man's life for his idea of the truth.

Yet, in the army, one is taught that killing is not only necessary but also acceptable. For example, part of the mission of the infantry is to "close with and destroy the enemy." An army attempts to strip soldiers of their reason and love, and substitute blind obedience and hatred for the "enemy" in their place. The My Lai tragedy demonstrates what can happen to individuals who are constantly told that killing other human beings is laudable. The fact that these men were serving their country at the time does not justify the massacre. In "Civil Disobedience," Thoreau states, "the mass of men serve the state thus, not as men mainly, but as machines, with their bodies...In most cases, there is no free exercise whatever of the judgement [sic] or of the moral sense; but they put themselves on a level with wood and earth and stones..." I cannot accept this; for me, the commandment "to love" overshadows the laws made by men. Thoreau also said, "I think we should be men first and subjects afterward." For me, to engage in killing other human beings would make me less than a man.

The pacifist attitude is often criticized as being too idealistic. The belief that idealism is the wrong attitude leads many to the conclusion that to live in any human society, one has to accept violence and war.

However, I cannot accept this attitude because I have faith in the essential goodness of man. Every man is made in the image of God, and as such has a tremendous potential for good; one need only listen to Handel's "Hallelujah Chorus" or pause before one of Picasso's paintings to be awed by the capacity for good that man has. There must come a time when this capacity can develop to its fullest extent, when men can substitute love and understanding for violence. Isaiah spoke of a time when "the wolf shall dwell with the lamb." Jerome Frank, a contemporary psychiatrist, states that "Surely if humans have the capacity to invent war, they have the capacity to invent substitutes for it." I have to believe that man was created for some greater good than killing other men. I believe that man does have the capacity to end wars and to live together peacefully. I believe that someday men will "beat their swords into plowshares" and nations will no longer make war.

—

For these reasons, I must request discharge from the Army as a conscientious objector.

b) Explain how, when, and from whom or from what sources the applicant received the training and acquired the belief which is the basis of claim: As long as I can remember, religion has been a part of my life. I attended church and Sunday school almost every Sunday when I lived at home. When I was eleven, I joined the Methodist Church in my hometown and took active part in it. During my senior year in high school, I was president of the local Methodist Youth Fellowship, and took part in church Bible study groups and discussions. Through this, I gained a belief in God and a basic knowledge and faith in the words of the New Testament. West Point had been a goal of mine for many years. There was much prestige attached to attending the military academy. Acceptance acknowledged superior allaround ability, and it provided a way to serve the country, which I believe every person should do. Thus, before I arrived, West Point seemed to offer everything worthwhile in an education.

I was somewhat surprised, then, to learn that I had to undergo training with a bayonet and shout enthusiastically that the spirit of the bayonet was "To kill, sir!" This was not exactly what I had expected, and it made me somewhat uneasy. However, at the time, actual combat duty was four years away, distant enough to make it seem less important than the day-to-day struggle of New Cadet Barracks. Also, I decided that I would not be an infantry officer, whose job emphasized the hand-to-hand combat portion of the Army. I believed that I could better serve in a branch not so close to the actual fighting. Finally, the positive aspects to be gained from a West Point education seemed more important that a few words I was required to say. I rationalized that if West Point required me to yell "To kill!" and to practice plunging my bayonet into an imaginary opponent, I had the duty because West Point was an ideal. Now I realize that all members of the Army, even those not engaged in actual combat, take part in the killing of others, since to be a member, even if a non-combatant role, is to condone the actions of the entire organization, which I cannot in conscience do. However, the uneasiness would sometimes return. I can remember being told in chapel that a soldier has the greatest moral responsibility of any person since he must take human life. Somehow, this statement seemed wrong because the Bible says "Thou shalt not kill" and "turn the other cheek." However, I assumed that a chaplain knew more than I did, and pushed the doubts to the back of my mind.

They did not surface again seriously until the summer between my sophomore and junior years. This time, I was on the teaching end of the bayonet, training incoming plebes to kill people. The beauty of the river and surrounding hills stood in sharp contrast to the savage growls of the new plebes, trying to emulate the "trained killer" on the demonstration platform. I wondered how many realized what they were doing.... But I couldn't dwell on such somber thoughts. I was a squad leader, with a role to play; I had to set the example for my eleven followers, and I figured that an example which rejected the goals they were trying to achieve was no example at all. Therefore, I closed my eyes to the brutality of the summer training to play the role expected of me. Reorganization came, then the first-day of Junior academics, and the question seemed permanently decided; I was now committed to the Army. I concluded that I would become either an Air Defense or Military Intelligence officer because these branches did not actually participate in the close combat. In September, I was not certain of what I believed; I only knew that much of Army duty was distasteful to me. By joining either of those two branches, I felt I could serve in the Army in a positive manner, without compromising my then-uncertain beliefs. I also planned to attend graduate school as soon as soon as possible after graduation. I felt that a graduate degree would qualify me for a position that did not involve direct combat.

However, in the fall I read "Siddhartha" by Hermann Hesse. This short novel describes a Buddhist's search for truth. He discovers that each part of the world is linked together, like the constant flow of a river; each drop is different, yet an integral part of the whole. This idea struck deep inside me and seemed to fit well with the New Testament teachings I knew. I also read J.D. Salinger's "Franny and Zooey" and "Raise High the Roofbeam, Carpenters," which say that each person, big or small, is an image of Christ, is Christ himself. My thoughts again turned to the value of human life.

At much the same time, the Vietnam moratoriums were held and the news of the My Lai incident broke, and both had a profound effect on me. These, coupled with the news that one of the boys I graduated from high school with had been killed in Vietnam, made me realize that people really die in wars: people who work and have families and pray and love—people, in effect, just like me; and I began to wonder why. The moratorium made me realize coldly that I was preparing for war and really nothing more. After four years of college, I would be able to lead men in combat; in addition, I was expected to look forward to it, and to enjoy it. Several professors said, "When you men get to Vietnam...," or "When you get your unit...."; for them, there was no concept of the war ending. My military science classes reinforced this thought. We were told that to take a hill we had to use certain procedures; for example, we should be certain of a three-to-one advantage in men before attacking, to insure a minimum level of casualties. I wondered how any casualty could be acceptable. Would the victim's wife, mother, or children find it acceptable? I recalled a story I had read, "The Most Dangerous Game," in which a famous hunter is shipwrecked on an inland inhabited by another hunter, one who has grown tired of conventional "big game" hunting. Instead, he hunts the men who are shipwrecked on his island. The reader is horrified at the low value placed on human life by the hunter; yet during war, in which the same type of behavior occurs, few people object. James Kunen has written the following: "Isn't it singular that no one ever goes to jail for waging wars, let alone advocating them? But the jails are filled with those who want peace. Not to kill is to be a criminal.... It strikes me as quite singular."

At first, these ideas frightened me; they were not only unconventional, they challenge the entire meaning of something I was committed to do. Yet, to me, war was contrary to Christ's commandments. Why, then, did so many people, nominally called Christians, advocate and support wars, which are direct violation of Christ's admonition to "love the neighbor"?

I discussed this matter with Chaplain Easterling and after much prayer and thought I concluded that there is no way to reconcile the concept of loving one's neighbor and war. One question still remained. Even though no one really wants war, isn't war sometimes necessary to defend the country? I cannot answer this question for everyone; however, I cannot accept a moral code or religion, which applies one standard for individuals and another for nations and individuals acting in behalf of nations. I am willing to work for the country; on the other hand, I do not believe that killing for the defense of the country justifies the killing. On a larger scale, if the whole world realized the futility and waste of war, then there would be no need for killing.

Obviously, 1 cannot speak for the whole world, but I must speak for myself, and my conscience calls on me to reject war as means to any end, and instead to substitute love. Perhaps this is not a logical decision in the world as it is; however, I do not consider war, which involves the destruction of man and of the world given to him, a logical choice either. To me, this is the only decision I can make, given the faith I have in God and man. In addition, I believe the world can and will be made a better place than it is at present. To reject war is to place my faith in the future. For me to participate in the Army, which has as its goal the winning of wars and the destruction of life, would be to reject the better future world. I am not rejecting service to my country; however, I do not believe that one must kill to serve his country. I believe service is important and necessary, but I want to make a positive contribution, to build rather than to destroy.

These decisions have not been easy to make. My family has discouraged them, and the questions they pose have been ignored during my three years at West Point.

However, in finally making them, I have been guided by the words of the Cadet Prayer: "Make us to choose the harder right instead of the easier wrong... and know no fear when truth and right are in jeopardy." For me, the harder right is to submit this request for discharge as a conscientious objector.

c) The name and present address of the individual upon whom the applicant relies most for religious guidance in matters of conviction relating to claim:

Chaplain Michael Easterling
7 Thayer Road
West Point, New York 10996

d) A statement as to circumstances, if any, under which the applicant believes the use of force:

Christ said, "I say unto you that ye resist not evil; but that whosoever smite thee on thy right cheek turn to him the other also...Love your enemies..."

A Quaker once wrote, "Force can restrain an evil man; only love can change him." I agree with these statements. I believe that force may be used when necessary to restrain someone from harming another when more love would be shown in preventing another from harm than by allowing him to be injured. For example, I believe that I would use force to protect my family from a burglar; on the other hand, I believe that only a minimum of force should be used.

There is a vast difference between violence of war and the protection of one's family. Whereas in the second case one acts from selfless love, during war men kill for the interests of their own nation. Instead of love, war breeds hatred and intolerance.

During a war, there is little attempt made to restrain the amount of force used. In Vietnam, soldiers of both sides do not hesitate to destroy whole villages to find a handful of the enemy. No matter how idealistic a nation's aims are, I do not believe they can be achieved by violence because violence cannot change the minds of people; it can only alienate them.

—

For these reasons, I can accept a minimum use of force only as a last resort to protect an individual from immediate harm.

e) A description of the actions and behavior in the applicant's life which, in his opinion, most conspicuously demonstrates the consistency and depth of religious conviction which gave rise to claim:

I acquired a belief in God early in life. I have been a regular church-attender since I can remember, and I joined the Methodist Church in New Baden, Illinois, at age eleven. During high school, I served as Vice-president, then President of the local Methodist Youth Fellowship, and took part in various other church activities. At West

Point, I attend church services during leave as well as while at the academy.

—

My beliefs concerning war have only recently crystallized, and at West Point, there are few opportunities to display such sentiment. However, my concern for the problem of war is shown by my seeking counsel on the subject; I have discussed war with a counselor and a chaplain, and have taken part in informal discussion groups organized by the Chaplain's Office. My concern for the problem of war is also shown in the following poem I wrote during the past year.

#1 silver mountain
 ghost of the evening
 have you come to
 disturb my peace? for
in your silver mirror
i see the wrinkled gray-
stone fortress before me
pounding his drum;
tramping soldiers rise
 from the green carpet at
its feet and their harsh
shouts mingle with the
 rolling thunder of the
terrible drum, driving
all the world watching
to his menacing
command but i can't
follow my feet won't
move; the drum calls
me it beckons but I am
frozen by its shadow
helplessly I just stand

and watch the thunder
of the terrible pounding
drum to watch I can
 never go-- from which I
cannot escape

—

The best demonstration of the sincerity of my beliefs is the submission of this application in spite of the objections of my parents. I plan in the future to work for peace and understanding among men, to try to bring about the better world that I envision, so that someday war might become as obsolete as dueling is now.

DISTRICT COURT DECISION

318 F.Supp. 126

United States District Court, S.D. New York.

UNITED STATES ex rel. Cary E. DONHAM,

Petitioner,

v.

Stanley R. RESOR, Secretary of the Army, et al., Respondents.

No. 70 Civ. 3363.

Sept. 3, 1970.

ATTORNEYS AND LAW FIRMS

*126 Rabinowitz, Boudin & Standard, New York City, for petitioner; Joan Goldberg, New York City, of counsel.

Whitney North Seymour, Jr., U.S. Atty. for Southern District of N.Y., New York City, for respondents; Michael I. Saltzman, Washington, D.C., of counsel.

OPINION

FRANKEL, District Judge.

Petitioner, at the end of his third year at West Point, sought separation from the Corps of Cadets on the ground that he had matured conscientious objections to military service. The Army has denied his application. He sues here for a writ of habeas corpus, claiming that the adverse decision of the military authorities lacked the requisite basis in fact.1

*127 The case appears to be the first in which a cadet has claimed the kind of dramatic change in outlook and ambition petitioner asserts. Apart from what this might be thought to symbolize about our world in more general terms, the uniqueness of the problem could have generated some finicky legal questions of both substance and procedure. But all concerned have concurred in adapting existing administrative procedures to petitioner's case, and it has been for the most part undisputed (but see note 2, infra) that substantive doctrines developed mainly in selective service cases are applicable. We proceed to the merits on this basis.

I.

As his brief observes, petitioner built in three full academic years, a 'splendid record at the military academy * * *.' He stood in the top fifth of his class. He was a squad leader in his junior year. So far as those in charge of his education and status were informed, he was completing successfully the training for a career as a professional army officer.

On May 29, 1970, however, he filed his application for discharge as a conscientious objector. In it he stated that his 'beliefs concerning war stem from a belief in God and in the New Testament teachings of Christ.' Citing

212

the New Testament and other writings, he wrote that he believed himself to have 'no right to take the life of any other person * * *.' 'Yet,' he continued, 'in the army, one is taught that killing is not only necessary but also acceptable. For example, part of the mission of the infantry is to 'close with and destroy the enemy." Quoting from Thoreau, psychiatrist Jerome Frank, and others, he went on to detail his commitment to love and peace and his rejection of war and killing.

He recounted his steady devotion since early childhood to the activities and doctrines of the Methodist Church. At the same time, he said, 'West Point has been a goal of mine for many years'— for the 'prestige,' because it 'provided a way to serve the country,' because, in sum, it 'seemed to offer everything worthwhile in an education.'

However, he continued, the reality of West Point was disturbing to him from the outset:

'I was somewhat surprised * * * to learn that I had to undergo training with a bayonet and shout enthusiastically that the spirit of the bayonet was 'To kill, sir.' This was not exactly what I had expected, and it made me somewhat uneasy. However, at the time, actual combat duty was four years away, distant enough to make it seem much less important than the day-to-day struggle of New Cadet Barracks. Also, I decided that I would not be an infantry officer, whose job emphasized the hand-to-hand combat portion of the Army. I believed that I could better serve in a branch not so close to the actual fighting. Finally, the positive aspects to be gained from a West Point education seemed more important that a few words I was required to say. * * * Now I realize that all members of the Army, even those not engaged in actual combat, take part in the killing of others, since to be a member, even in a non-combatant role, is to condone the actions of the entire organization, which I cannot in conscience do.'

Petitioner went on in his application to describe how the doubts 'would sometimes return;' how he 'pushed (them) to the back of (his) mind;' and how they 'did not surface again seriously until the summer between (his) sophomore and junior years.' I that summer, almost a year before his filing of the instant application, he 'was on the teaching end of the bayonet, training incoming plebes to kill people.' Once more he found himself thinking 'sombre thoughts,' but again he 'closed (his) eyes' and went on with his duties as squad leader. He concluded that he would serve in a branch of the army which 'did not actually participate in the close combat.' By September of that year, he stated, he was 'not certain of what (he) believed; (he) only knew that much of Army duty was distasteful to (him).'

During the fall he continued his readings, his application said. Then, the Vietnam moratorium and 'the news of the Mylai incident * * * both had a profound effect on (him). These, coupled with the news that one of the boys (he) graduated from high school with had been killed in Vietnam, made (him) realize that people really die in wars * * * and (he) began to wonder why.' He was now made to 'realize coldly' that he was being prepared for war, and that 'after four years of college, (he) would be able to lead men in combat * * *.' He also found himself recoiling from the realization that he was expected to enjoy his career in combat. He says he found himself 'frightened' and confused by these ideas. He discussed them with the chaplain. He prayed and thought a great deal. Then, he 'concluded that there is no way to reconcile the concept of loving one's neighbor and war.' After describing a course of further thought and soul-searching, the application stated, the petitioner concluded that his conscience called upon him 'to reject war as a means to any end, and instead to substitute love.'

The remainder of the application, though all of it is relevant, may be more briefly summarized. Petitioner went on to describe the limited degree to which he might believe in the use of force. He amplified his description of the course of his religious thought and beliefs, setting out some poems he had written during the preceding year or so as reflective of the cast of his mind. He noted that the application he was now presenting was opposed by his parents, and urged this among other things as a demonstration of the sincerity of his beliefs. As to whether he had ever 'given public expression' to the views now stated, he said these views had 'been expressed only in private conversations and writings.'

Accompanying the application were letters from petitioner's hometown pastor, a high school teacher and coach, roommates at the Military Academy, instructors at a local college near the Academy, and others. All attested to the petitioner's integrity, honesty and sincerity.

The Assistant Chaplain of the Academy submitted his views on the application. He stated that he believed Cadet Donham 'to be sincere in his convictions and to be a young man of integrity.'

As a further step in the procedure, the petitioner was seen for psychiatric evaluation. The Chief of the Academy's neuropsychiatric service reported that he suffered from no 'emotional disturbance or psychiatric disease.' In addition, while recognizing that it was 'not the purpose of (his) office to judge the sincerity of validity of Conscientious Objector arguments,' the medical officer wrote that 'it would nevertheless appear warranted to state that Cadet Donham's convictions are based on considerable reasoning and cogent thought processes.'

On June 16, 1970, petitioner appeared before Lt. Col. J. E. Gleason for a personal interview on his application. Counsel for petitioner attended with him and made a transcript of the conversation which was later before the ultimate decision-makers in the military hierarchy and before this court. Petitioner on this occasion summarized orally the beliefs stated at greater lenth in his written application. He was asked by Colonel Gleason to 'name * * * all' the writers to whom the application referred and to tell how they had affected his beliefs. In answer to other questions *129 he said that he had tried to read on both sides of the subject before reaching his ultimate conclusion. He told once more about his doubts long before the time of his application and about his successful quelling of them while he went on through the completion of the third academic year. When asked whether he had considered that he was compromising himself, he said that he believed 'this was something (he) would get use to.' Continuing on the subject of the delay in reporting his feelings of conscience, the interview summary of petitioner's counsel contains the following colloquy:

'Col. Gleason: When did you indicate to chain of command that this was the course of action you had decided to take? 'Mr. Donham: After final examinations.

'Col. Gleason: Why did you wait until after the final examinations?

'Mr. Donham: I did not know whether I would be permitted to finish the school year.'

The interview with Colonel Gleason proceeded to other matters not necessary to recount in detail. At the conclusion the Colonel observed that he was 'still not satisfied that Mr. Donham is opposed to all war.' He volunteered his 'own feeling * * * that an army is necessary in order to keep the peace and this is the main purpose of the army.'

Colonel Gleason then prepared a report dated June 18,

1970, concerning the interview with petitioner and the Colonel's conclusions and recommendations. He recommended disapproval. He noted that the petitioner's decision to seek discharge as a conscientious objector had been reached in February, 1970, and reported then, in confidence, to a cadet counsellor. He recounted further that petitioner had retained civilian legal assistance in March, and then noted that the request for discharge had not been submitted until the end of May. He emphasized the petitioner's explanation that the delay was motivated by his desire to obtain academic credit for the courses taken in his third year. The Colonel found that the 'delay indicates insincerity, as on one hand he states he cannot serve in the Army, even as a non-combatant, yet he willfully, for personal advancement, remained associated with the Academy and actively participated in all training for approximately four months subsequent to his decision.'

Colonel Gleason went on to express his view (excluded in the final decision) that petitioner 'has not developed his claimed convictions through religious training and beliefs.' He criticized the adequacy of petitioner's knowledge about the literary sources to which the application referred. He suggested that petitioner had first chosen to claim conscientious objector status 'and then sought literary material to support the decision.'

Then, reporting on the question of when petitioner might think force appropriate, the Colonel summarized his questions to petitioner about World War II and, specifically, the killing of Jews during that conflict. The

Colonel gave it as his impression that petitioner 'would not have been opposed to participation in that war.'

Colonel Gleason expressed his opinion that petitioner's 'decision stems from an objection to the Vietnam war because of the personal risks that are now apparent and real.' He noted that the beliefs expressed in petitioner's application had not been expressed or claimed through the years of military training, including intensive training as both student and teacher in techniques of killing in combat. He commented unfavorably upon petitioner's recent hope that he could avoid the problem by attending graduate school and seeking an assignment to some area of the service not involved in combat.

Proceeding through military channels, petitioner's application was next considered by the Commandant of Cadets. That official recommended to the Superintendent that the application be denied *130 on the ground that it was 'prompted not by any sincere, bonafide, deep-rooted conviction but by (petitioner's) desire to avoid obligated service.' On the next day the Superintendent concurred in the recommendation of disapproval and sent the file along to the Department of the Army.

The final and authoritative decision was made and reported in a written opinion of July 21, 1970, by the Department of the Army's Conscientious Objector Review Board. The Board held that petitioner's application must be denied. The exclusive ground of this determination was the conclusion that petitioner 'lacks the depth of sincerity to qualify for discharge as a conscientious objector * * *.' This finding, the opinion states, 'is based on an objective analysis of facts found in the record.' The Board found that petitioner's fundamental beliefs on the subject of central concern were not essentially different now from what they had been when he first entered the

Academy. It emphasized petitioner's repeated references to his interest in obtaining a West Point education. The Board observed that 'it appears from the record that this fact has apparently had a strong influence on the timing of (petitioner's) declaration of conscientious objection.' The Board quoted at some length from the passages in petitioner's application expressing his surprise to learn that he would undergo training in the Military Academy in the techniques of killing people in wartime. It quoted the passages where petitioner expressed his long-held hope that he could or would arrange to serve in some non-combatant capacity. The Board found that the initial failure of the petitioner to make his doubts 'known to the proper officials' was at first 'fully understandable,' but that 'his continued failure to express such growing feelings for over a period of two and one-half years makes his motives in not doing so suspect.'

Returning to the repeated statements of petitioner that he planned to serve in areas outside of combat, the Board found that these 'self-serving plans and aspirations cast * * * doubt as to the reason for his delay in expressing what (he) claims were long-held feelings.' The Board quoted the passage in his application where petitioner told of the growing disturbance in his mind over the conflict in Vietnam and his personal acquaintance with a young man killed there, emphasizing the following sentences:

'* * * The moratorium made me realize coldly that I was preparing for war and really nothing more. After four years of college, I would be able to lead men in combat; in addition, I was expected to look forward to it, and enjoy it.'

Commenting on the quoted words and others to the same tenor in petitioner's application, the Board said:

'* * * The naivete of these statements, coming from an intelligent young man who had already spent two years at West Point, creates further doubt as to the extent to which his beliefs are truly held. As expressed in Parrott v. United States: 'An average man of average intelligence who can read must daily realize that he may, once he is subject to a draft call from his local board * * * be soon called upon to kill.' A U.S. Military Academy cadet who has spent over two years at the Academy certainly cannot be equated in knowledge of such matters with an average draftee, who conceivably might not know about the more necessary (albeit unpleasant and unfortunate) aspects of Army duty. Coming from a man with Donham's background, this statement is simply not believable.'

The Board then referred in a similar vein to the colloquy (quoted supra) from the interview transcript prepared by petitioner's counsel where he explained the reasons for his delay from March to May in filing his application. The Board stressed in this quotation petitioner's statement that he was concerned about whether 'he would be permitted *131 to finish the school year.' Regarding this, the Board said:

'* * * The * * * quotation clearly indicates that Donham's professed beliefs are not deeply held. Although his doubts about serving in the Army and participating in war (which had begun early in his stay at West Point) had finally led Donham to the conclusion that he was required beyond all doubt by his conscience to request discharge, he did not hold his beliefs so strongly that he could not wait until the end of the semester, so that he could obtain credit for the full academic year. It would seem that if Donham held his beliefs as deeply as he professes, he would have felt bound to apply at the time he made his decision. Thus, he appears to have been more concerned with earning credit for his schooling than in following the dictates of his conscience. This theme runs throughout Donham's narrative description of the acquisition of his beliefs. His goal was to obtain an education.'

In sum, upon the single ground that petitioner had not displayed the requisite sincerity in his asserted convictions, the Board rendered the decision of disapproval which has been followed by his application to this court for a writ of habeas corpus.

II.

Petitioner's counsel has argued that the full record of his views— not excluding the doubts, the evidences of what the Board called naivete, and even the seemingly calculated delay in making his application— is consistent with the deep sincerity he has been held by the Army Board to lack. The substantial point is made that petitioner's candor in stating facts permitting adverse inferences is not the least of the factors in his favor. The brief for petitioner stresses the 'long list of reference letters (indicating) that people who have known petitioner most of his life, as well as those who have become acquainted with him more recently, believe that he is honest and sincere, a young man of deep convictions and a person who is not afraid to stand by his beliefs.' Perhaps less cogent, but at least piquant, is the contention that petitioner's 'splendid record at the military academy, which operates under an honor system, is further evidence of his integrity.'

[1]Taking them all together, petitioner's arguments might prevail if this court were commissioned to decide independently his application for discharge from West Point as a conscientious objector. But the court's role is a far more straitened one. As stated in petitioner's main brief, the judicial function here 'is the limited one of determining whether there was a basis in fact for finding that he was not a conscientious objector * * *.'2 More

specifically, the question is whether the Conscientious Objector Review Board could rationally and honestly have concluded from the facts before it that petitioner *132 had not demonstrated the requisite sincerity of his asserted convictions. United States v. Corliss, 280 F.2d 808, 814-815 (2d Cir.), cert. denied, 364 U.S. 884, 81 S.Ct. 167, 5 L.Ed.2d 105 (1960).

 Thus understood, the problem is not a difficult one. The Board cannot be held to have been irrational or itself insincere when it found on this record an insufficient basis for finding petitioner sincere in his professed views.

[2][3] While sincerity 'is, of course, a question of fact,'

United States v. Seeger, 380 U.S. 163, 185, 85 S.Ct. 850, 13 L.Ed.2d 733 (1965), it is a complex and subtle one on which no single 'fact' is likely to be decisive. There are, nevertheless, indicia taught by the general experience of men and the specific run of cases touching the area of present concern. Prudence and circumspection in revealing beliefs about fundamental things need not necessarily reflect a lack of sincerity. Here, however, while petitioner postponed disclosure, he continued to serve in an establishment and learn and teach things he then claimed to find intolerable as a matter of conscience and basic conviction. The Board was not irrational when it counted heavily against petitioner the delay (including the final period for completing his third year's work) in submitting his application. This is not the first case in which long delay, unimpressively explained, has been a factor adverse to claims like petitioner's. Cf., e.g., United States v. Messinger, 413 F.2d 927, 930, 932 (2d Cir. 1969), cert. denied, 399 U.S. 927, 90 S.Ct. 2230, 26 L.Ed.2d 792 (1970); Paszel v. Laird, 426 F.2d 1169, 1175 (2d Cir. 1970); Salamy v. United States, 379 F.2d 838, 842 (10th Cir.1967).

The Board was not less within the realm of allowable judgment when it weighed against petitioner the notable length of time he claimed to have required to comprehend the nature and purpose of his West Point training. His initial reaction to West Point in this era of movies and television— that he was 'somewhat surprised * * * to learn that (he) had to undergo training with a bayonet'— could have been in itself hard for the Board to swallow. His later assertion that it took him over two years at the Academy to 'realize that people really die in wars' was held to be an incredible assertion of naivete. Petitioner's counsel treats these and other statements of like tenor with the observation that we recognize today the frequently large gap between intellectual and emotional 'understanding.' The *133 court accepts the point as a substantial one. The Board, however, was not required to treat it as either a sufficient or even a very weighty one in all the circumstances of this case. The Board was permitted to conclude, as it did, that the asserted lack of sophistication of this intelligent cadet exposed a level of disingenuousness incompatible with his profession of sincerity.

The other details supportive of the military decision are adequately stated in the precisely circumscribed opinion of the Board. Considering its decision as a whole upon the record as a whole, the court finds that the result here assailed stands firmly upon the required basis in fact. [4] A section of petitioner's posthearing memorandum (pp. 21-22) asserts that the Review Board's decision must be nullified because it misses the 'proper standard' when, instead of saying 'petitioner lacks sincerity,' it says he 'lacks the depth of sincerity to qualify for discharge.' (Petitioner's emphasis.) The reference to 'depth,' petitioner says, is a mistaken importation of an unconstitutionally vague criterion. The argument is not substantial.

The notion of 'depth' of conviction is neither novel nor questionable in this context. To cite only a recent reminder from the Supreme Court, the

223

central concern relates either to traditionally religious beliefs, like those petitioner professes, or at least to 'beliefs * * * held with the strength of traditional religious convictions.' Welsh v. United States, 398 U.S. 333, 340, 90 S.Ct. 1792, 1796, 26 L.Ed.2d 308 (1970). It is apt, therefore, as the same opinion reflects, in judging the 'strength' with which beliefs are held, to state the question and answer in terms of whether the 'individual deeply and sincerely holds' the beliefs. Id. Far from being a mistake or a novelty, it is sound and familiar to identify the vital quality of conviction in terms of 'sincerity and depth' (id. at 337, 90 S.Ct. 1792), 'strength' (id.), whether the beliefs are 'sincere and meaningful' (id. at 339, 90 S.Ct. 1792) and 'deeply held' (id. at 344, 90 S.Ct. 1792). See also id. at 342, 343, 90 S.Ct. 1792.

It seems clear without more that petitioner's attack upon the Board's choice of words is a waste of time. Beyond the abstractly semantic terms in which the argument is presented, the context supplies more thorough refutation. The Board revealed pervasively that its focus was correct. It expressed its judgment that petitioner's 'motives (were) suspect;' it identified specific grounds for doubting his stated reasons for delaying his application; it found in this aspect of the record evidence that his beliefs were 'not deeply held;' it noted his 'naivete' about what West Point taught, and found this a basis for 'further doubt as to the extent to which his beliefs are truly held;' it judged his assertion about the time it took him to 'realize' this to be 'simply not believable.' The Board, like the Supreme Court, repeatedly indicated the test as being how 'strongly' or 'deeply' petitioner held his asserted beliefs, and found his application insufficient in these terms. The supposed defect in its phraseology is in no sense a substantial point.

For the above reasons, the petition for a writ of habeas corpus is denied.

So ordered.

All Citations 318 F.Supp. 126

Footnotes

[1] Both sides agree that this ultimate contention is now ripe for decision upon the record before the court. Arguable questions about the court's
jurisdiction have been foregone by the government, reflecting a view the
court finds sound. See United States ex rel. Brooks v. Cliford, 409 F.2d
700, 706-707 (4th Cir. 1969), collecting cases from the Second and other
Circuits.

> As the case originally came on for the present decision,
> petitioner was seeking to enjoin proceedings for his sepa-
> ration upon grounds of insufficient 'aptitude' (i.e., unsuit-
> able attitude) for commissioning as an army officer. It has
> become common ground, however, that the injunction
> motion is academic. That would be patently true if habeas
> were granted. It is equally true under the decision herein
> denying the petition; petitioner plans in this situation to
> tender his resignation, and the government has stated that
> it will be accepted.

[2] That familiar standard of sharply restricted review derives from selective service cases. E.g., Estep v. United States, 327 U.S. 114, 122-123, 66
S.Ct. 423, 90 L.Ed. 567 (1946). Both sides joined originally in proposing its
application here.

Then, however, counsel for petitioner asked leave to file a post-hearing
memorandum on points she said were first confronted in the government's
opposing papers. Granted such leave, she argued some things for which
leave had been sought, then added as a final point an argument (available)

from the outset, but now substituted for the flatly contrary position there-tofore taken) that the 'no basis-in-fact' standard is unconstitutional as applied to her client. The argument is rejected.

Another contention raised for the first time in the post-hearing memoran-dum— and likewise entirely outside the area for which such a memoran-dum was allowed— is that the Army violated its own regulations because the papers forwarded to Washington lacked a recommendation from peti-tioner's 'unit commander.' The government understandably objects to con-sideration of this afterthought at all, but amply refutes it in any event.

[3] Petitioner's counsel focuses primarily on the vulnerabilities in what Colonel Gleason wrote and said. If the Colonel's expressions constituted the decision to be reviewed (or, what is the same thing, had the decision been for him to make), petitioner would stand on high ground. That is not the case, however, and it is not useful to discuss the seeming misconceptions in what the Colonel wrote. The decision of the Board, deliberately complete and sharply limited to the single ground now in issue, appears explicitly to avoid the Colonel's disputed observations. At any rate, it neither adopts nor is in any way impaired by them. Cf. United States v. Bornemann, 424 F.2d 1343, 1348-1349 (2d Cir. 1970); United States v. Messinger, 413 F.2d 927, 930-931 (2d Cir. 1969).

Petitioner's position in this respect is not enhanced by the variant formu-lation that the Army violated its own regulation, Department of Defense Directive 1300.6 (May 10, 1968), which provides that the officer in Colonel Gleason's role should be one 'knowledgeable in policies and procedures relating to conscientious objector matters.' No question of this sort was raised before or during the interview with Colonel Gleason. He was qual-ified by rank and by his membership in the Adjutant General's Corps, which normally is charged with such duties. See Reitemeyer v. McCrea, 302 F.Supp. 1210, 1217-1218 n. 5 (D.Md.1969). The argument now made is said to derive support from the fact that the Colonel made legal errors, including an asserted misinterpretation of a Supreme Court decision announced three days before the date of his report. Even for judicial officers, with power to decide authoritatively (unlike the Colonel), it is not the law that errors are disqualifying in the impossible sense of petitioner's theory.

APPELLATE COURT DECISION

436 F.2d 751

United States Court of Appeals, Second Circuit.

UNITED STATES ex rel. Cary E. DONHAM,

Petitioner-Appellant,

v.

Stanley R. RESOR, Secretary of the Army, and

Major General William Knowlton, Superintendent, United States Military Academy, West Point, New York, Respondents-Appellees.

No. 387, Docket 35512.

|

Argued Dec. 3, 1970.

|

Decided Jan. 6, 1971.

Attorneys and Law Firms

*752 Joan Goldberg, Rabinowitz, Boudin & Standard, New York City (Victor Rabinowitz, New York City, National Emergency Civil Liberties Committee, of counsel), for petitioner-appellant.

Michael I. Saltzman, Asst. U.S. Atty. (Whitney North Seymour, Jr., U.S. Atty. S.D.N.Y., of counsel), for respondents-appellees.

Before FRIENDLY, SMITH and ANDERSON, Circuit Judges.

Opinion

J. JOSEPH SMITH, Circuit Judge

Petitioner, a cadet at West Point, sought separation from the Academy at the end of his third year because he had become a conscientious objector. A cadet may not withdraw from the Academy after his second year without incurring an immediate military duty requirement unless excused by separation as a conscientious objector. The Army rejected his conscientious objector claims on the grounds that his beliefs lacked the necessary depth of sincerity. Petitioner brought an action in the United States District Court for the Southern District of New York for a writ of habeas corpus, attacking both the substance of and procedure leading up to the Army's decision. The court, Marvin E. Frankel, Judge, denied the writ. We find error and reverse and remand with instructions to stay active duty orders pending further proceedings by the Army.

The points in issue on appeal are, basically, three: what is the applicable standard of judicial review; was the Army's decision supportable under the correct standard; and in any case, did *753 the Army fail to follow its own regulations, to the prejudice of petitioner.

It has long been established that the proper standard of review in Selective Service cases has been whether the deciding body had any basis in fact for its decision. Estep v. United States, 327 U.S. 114, 122-123, 66 S.Ct. 423, 90 L.Ed. 567 (1946). Originally, it seems that both sides in this case accepted the application of that standard here. However, petitioner, subsequent to the initial hearing in the district court, argued that the 'no basis-in-fact' standard is unconstitutional as applied here, and that the proper standard of review is the one familiar in the administrative law area, 'substantial evidence.' Judge Frankel rejected the argument. Petitioner argues that although the standard may be constitutional in the Selective Service area, it is not when applied to an in-service conscientious objector applicant. This is so because 'all of the officers conducting interviews and making decisions are in the Army, and there is no right to appeal from the Army determination.' It is contended that the Army officer who hears the applicant's case generally possesses views that 'concededly do not embrace conscientious objection and whose very position in the Army may make it impossible for him to be objective.' In Selective Service cases, on the other hand, the local board consists of volunteer civilians, and there is a right of appeal to the State Appeal Board. This argument, however, is based on unproven assumptions. We cannot say that fair determination is not possible within the military, and the Army regulations themselves are designed to provide it. However, even though the standard is the same as in draft cases, and review is limited to the narrow issue of whether there is a basis in fact for the Army determination, the courts have, of course, required the Army to base its findings upon objective evidence.1

In any case, petitioner argues that there was no basis in fact for the Army's decision. This claim we must reject.

U. S. ex rel. Donham v. Resor, 436 F.2d 751 (1971)

Judge Frankel expressed the opinion that if he had been commissioned to decide independently petitioner's application for discharge, petitioner's arguments might have prevailed. Judge Frankel felt, however, that given the court's more limited role, he was forced to uphold the Army's decision, since there did exist a basis in fact to support it. Were there complete compliance with the Army requirements in reaching the determination, we would be constrained to agree.

Petitioner filed his application for discharge on May 29, 1970. He stated that his 'beliefs concerning war stem from a belief in God and in the New Testament teachings of Christ.' He believed that he had no right to take the life of any other person, yet in the Army, one is taught that killing is not only necessary but is also acceptable. He said his beliefs stemmed from childhood, but, somewhat surprisingly, he went on to note that 'West Point has been a goal of mine for many years,' for the prestige, because it provided a way to serve his country and because it 'seemed to offer everything worthwhile in an education.' Although the bayonet training was disturbing at the outset, he pushed it to the back of his mind.

*754 It was a combination of several factors, petitioner claimed, that combined to cause his ultimate 'crystallization.' First, when he was called upon to teach plebes the use of the bayonet, he found himself thinking 'somber thoughts.' Secondly, the Vietnam moratorium of that fall and news of the My Lai incident 'both had a profound effect' on him. Finally, the news that one of the boys with whom he had gone to high school was killed in Vietnam made him realize that people really die in wars. A number of those with intimate contacts with Donham certified to the sincerity and depth of his evolving scruples of conscience.

[3] In accord with Army regulations, petitioner was interviewed by a chaplain, a psychiatrist, and an Army officer. Both the chaplain and the psychiatrist expressed the view that petitioner was sincere in his convictions and a man of integrity. The Army officer, Lt. Col. Gleason, however, felt quite differently. Colonel Gleason's major concern was the fact that petitioner had waited until after final examinations his third year to file his application, even though he admitted that his beliefs against war had crystallized at least several months earlier. At his interview with Colonel Gleason, petitioner candidly admitted that he waited until after final examinations because 'I did not know whether I would be permitted to finish the school year.' Judge Frankel concluded that the Army's decision had a basis in fact, since 'while petitioner postponed disclosure, he continued to serve in an establishment and learn and teach things he then claimed to find intolerable as a matter of conscience and basic conviction.' We agree that this provided a basis in fact for the Army's decision.

However, the Army's determination can stand only if it was arrived at in pursuance of the law and regulations, and there we differ with the court below.

Department of Defense Directive 1300.6 VI.B.4 requires the hearing officer who hears the applicant requesting discharge to be 'knowledgeable in policies and procedures relating to conscientious objector matters.' Petitioner cites numerous instances of Colonel Gleason's total lack of knowledge concerning conscientious objection. He found that the applicant's religion must advocate conscientious objection, although this had apparently not been the law since the First World War. He was not aware of the elimination of religious requirements for conscientious objection. Moreover, Colonel Gleason apparently lacked the necessary objectivity to be a fair, knowledgeable hearing officer. He obviously and no doubt honestly could not believe that a West Point cadet could possibly develop conscientious scruples against war and assumed more the role of advocate than judge.

The government argues, however, that Colonel Gleason was not the one to make the final decision on petitioner's application. Further, that those making the ultimate decision disregarded Colonel Gleason's findings concerning petitioner's lack of religious convictions and concerning his opposition to the Vietnam war, as opposed to all war. Yet if all three officers who had seen and heard petitioner (i.e., the psychiatrist and the chaplain who interviewed him and the hearing officer who observed him) had found petitioner sincere, the Army would have been hard pressed to justify its finding of insincerity (cf. United States ex rel. Tobias v. Laird, 413 F.2d 936 (4 Cir. 1969)), where the court, in overturning the Army's refusal to discharge the petitioner on conscientious objector grounds, emphasized that all three officers making recommendations recommended classification as a conscientious objector. 'We think the Army's own directives demonstrate a policy of reasonable common sense fairness to its soldiers— which policy has not been followed in this case.' 413 F.2d at 940. See also, United States ex rel. Brooks v. Clifford, 409 F.2d 700, 706 (4 Cir. 1969): 'Such regulations (for discharge of conscientious objectors) once issued must be followed scrupulously.'

*755 Moreover, the failure to include a recommendation by Donham's unit commanding officer was violative of the

233

Army's own regulations, which provide that recommendations will be forwarded to department headquarters. The unit commander is required by regulation (Army Regulation 635-20 P4635-20 P4.b(4) 1.) to make a recommendation. Major Baker, petitioner's tactical officer (who petitioner contends is the unit commander) failed to make the required recommendation, though he submitted the reports of the chaplain and psychiatrist and other required forms. The government contends that the petitioner's unit commander for the purposes of the regulations was the commandant of cadets or the superintendent of West Point, who did make the appropriate recommendations.

[4] Petitioner's contention appears to us correct. While 10 U.S.C. § 4334(b) and (c) provide that the superintendent is the commanding officer of the Academy and of the military post at West Point, and that the commandant of cadets is the immediate commander of the Corps of Cadets, § 4349(a) provides that the Corps of Cadets shall be divided into companies and that each company shall be commanded by a commissioned officer of the Army. For the purpose of the regulation the unit commander would appear to be the company commander. The obvious purpose of the regulation requiring a recommendation from the unit commander is to obtain an opinion from someone in close personal contact with the applicant. Clearly the company commander is in a far better position for this than the commandant who has the entire Corps of Cadets under his general supervision. The company commander's recommendation should be obtained and a hearing officer knowledgeable in accordance with regulations appointed.

We reverse and remand with instructions to stay Donham's orders to active military duty pending further proceedings by the Army in accord herewith.

All Citations 436 F.2d 751

FOOTNOTES

[1] See, for example, United States ex rel. Brooks v. Clifford, 409 F.2d 700, 707 (4 Cir. 1969), in which it was held that although the scope of review was sharply limited to determining whether there was a basis in fact for the Army's decision rejecting an enlisted man's conscientious objector claim, 'The fact that petitioner delayed the assertion of his claim until after his views had been formulated and that that did not occur until after his military service had begun and he had completed basic training and advanced or special weapon training is no ground to deny him discharge * * * if in reality his views are sincerely held and are the result of religious training and belief.'

End of Document